Dear Parts

Dear Parts

A Memoir of Trauma,

Psychedelic Healing,

and

Coming Home to Myself

By Kimberly Taylor D.O.

PUBLISHING

Hardcover ISBN: 979-8-9939632-0-4
Paperback ISBN: 979-8-9939632-1-1
E-ISBN: 979-8-9939632-2-8
Library of Congress Control Number: 2026901545

CLS Publishing
Wichita, Kansas
info@clspublishing.com

All of the events in this memoir are true to the best of the author's memory and reflect her own interpretation of them. They should not be taken as the beliefs or memories of any other person in the book. The reader should consider this book a work of literature based on real events.

Book design by Stacey Aaronson
Printed in the USA

This book is dedicated to the memory of Safia Lyon, APRN

*You were a gentle and steady presence in my journey.
Love and light were your constant companions and your
greatest gift. Now they remain, carrying your presence
into all those who follow. May my journey reflect the love
and light you so generously shared.*

AUTHOR'S NOTE

This book wasn't planned. It arrived.

I've been on a healing path for more than fifteen years. What started as a slow burn to find more meaning in life turned into a personal reckoning after a life-altering medical diagnosis. The last three years have been marked by an intense and transformative dive into trauma work, parts work, psychedelic-assisted therapy, and somatic healing. A desire to feel better physically, emotionally, and spiritually has slowly become a relationship with my internal world—one part at a time.

I have long thought I had a story to tell. But until recently, that story was stuck in my head. Then, something shifted.

The letters and reflections in this book were written over the course of only a few weeks, but they are the result of more than a decade of deep, often invisible, work. They emerged because my system was finally ready to speak, and I was finally ready to listen.

If you've been on a healing path and ever felt like it was taking too long or that your progress was invisible, I hope this book reminds you: nothing is wasted. The work you're doing now might be building the foundation for a powerful healing moment you can't yet imagine.

It's time we tell the truth about the things that live in the shadows. The things we carry—impulses, patterns, shutdowns, and shame—aren't signs that we're broken. They're signs that something happened.

As Richard Schwartz says, there are no bad parts, only parts that learned to survive in ways that may no longer serve us.

Even harmful behaviors are not who we are—they're adaptations to what happened to us. We've been taught to hide these parts. To feel ashamed of what makes us human.

But what if the very things we're most afraid to reveal are the ones that most deserve compassion?

There is nothing to be ashamed of. Not the mess. Not the coping. Not the silence, or the rage, or the need.

This book isn't a neat little "I healed, and here's how you can too" self-help book. There are plenty of those. This book is an unfiltered look at my process in real time. It includes illness, grief, loneliness, and even passive suicidal ideation. But also self-discovery, resilience, and hope.

It's messy. It's beautiful. It's everything in between.

If this book does anything, I hope it normalizes the truth that healing begins the moment we stop pretending we don't need it.

This isn't the story of someone who healed and then wrote a book. It's the story of someone who started writing when healing made it possible to speak—and who finally stopped pretending.

My healing is well underway, but in many ways, it has only just begun.

—Kim Taylor

HOW TO READ THIS BOOK

For many years, I didn't have words for how I felt. But I did have music. Even now, music still expresses what lives beyond language. Music has also been a trusted companion. It makes me feel less alone.

The songs in this book aren't random. They were pulled from personal playlists from some of the most difficult and meaningful moments of my life. Some artists appear multiple times—Sia, Shinedown, Mary Chapin Carpenter, and Sarah Bareilles—because their music has been a constant companion.

Some songs speak through the melody. Others speak through the lyrics, saying how I feel better than I can. All are here to support emotional connection, not just storytelling. Though no lyrics are reproduced due to copyright laws, song titles and artists are referenced for thematic context, and lyrics are readily available on the internet. Additionally, all songs are referenced by chapter in the appendix.

Below are the QR codes that link to the playlist for this book. Feel free to scan your preferred streaming platform now so you can listen to the songs as you read and let them move through you and deepen your experience.

Apple Music

Spotify

Amazon Music

There are also a few links to short video clips from my ketamine sessions. I include these to offer a deeper glimpse into what this work can look like. A word of caution: some of the content may be triggering. I encourage you to listen to your own nervous system and simply skip them if you find watching them too provocative.

This isn't a typical "self-help" book, with exercises at the end of each chapter, but rather a self-reflection experience—an invitation to travel with me on my journey and reflect on your own as you go. Notice where you see yourself in my story. Perhaps there will be some new awareness. Or maybe a shared experience of an old one will help you feel less alone.

Take your time. Read the words. Listen to the music. Notice what stirs in you. Journal. Cry. Create your own playlist. Give yourself compassion along the way.

This book includes honest reflections on suicidal thoughts, emotional numbness, and the desire to give up—because those moments are part of my story and part of many people's healing journeys.

If you're in a place where reading about these topics feels overwhelming, please take care of yourself. Pause, skip ahead, or put the book down. Your safety matters more than finishing what's written in these pages.

This book is not a substitute for professional support. If you are struggling or in crisis, reach out to a therapist, a trusted friend, or a crisis line. You are not too much. You don't have to carry it alone. There is nothing shameful in admitting you need help.

If you're in the US, you can call or text 988 Suicide & Crisis Lifeline or visit 988lifeline.org for 24/7 free and confidential support. For those outside the US, visit findahelpline.com to locate support in your country.

Lastly, I want to say welcome to my world. I got my invitation to the lunatic ball—and it's okay, because all of my readers got one too.

We're all just human. Beautifully, messily, resiliently human.

"Symptom of Being Human"
–Shinedown

This song reminds us that awkwardness, shame,
and feeling out of place are not flaws —
they're part of the shared human experience.

A BRIEF WORD ABOUT
THE MODALITIES

Throughout this book, I reference several therapeutic modalities that have been central to my healing. While the heart of this story is about relationships—between parts, with my therapist, with others, and with myself—these approaches provided the framework, tools, and containers that made the work possible. For those unfamiliar, here's a brief overview:

Internal Family Systems (IFS)

IFS is a therapy model developed by Dr. Richard Schwartz that sees each person as having a system of "parts"—distinct sub-personalities with their own roles, feelings, and needs. When trauma happens, these parts take on roles they weren't meant to in order to protect us from the pain.

We all have parts that carry burdens of prior traumas, abandonment, etc. Because these parts get exiled from the system, he calls these parts exiles. There are also Manager parts that serve to protect us from the pain within the exiles. An example is the inner critic or workaholic. Managers tend to distract us from ourselves.

Then there are the firefighters. These parts come in to put out the "fire"—the pain that gets triggered. Addictions are a result of a firefighter part.

Underneath all of the parts is a core Self (with a capital S) that can lead with qualities like compassion and clarity. In IFS, healing happens not by erasing parts, but by listening to them and helping them unburden what they carry. The ultimate goal is to lead from Self.

Ketamine-Assisted Psychotherapy (KAP)

KAP combines the dissociative medicine ketamine with psychotherapy to support deep emotional exploration and healing. In my experience, ketamine helped quiet my protective parts just enough for exiled emotions and sensations to emerge. It also opened space for Self energy to arise—making it possible to connect with parts I couldn't access otherwise.

Psychedelic Somatic Interactional Psychotherapy (PSIP)

PSIP is a body-based, trauma-informed method that uses low-dose psychedelics to help the nervous system process implicit memory—trauma held in the body rather than in words. Instead of guiding the experience verbally, the therapist tracks the body's movements, expressions, and energy, allowing deep survival responses to emerge and integrate. PSIP often brought me to the edge of raw sensation, where trauma lived, and helped me learn how to stay present with it.

Somatic Experiencing (SE)

Developed by Dr. Peter Levine, SE is a method of working with trauma through the body rather than through storytelling. It focuses on noticing sensations, movements, and impulses in the nervous system to allow for the completion of survival responses that were interrupted during trauma. SE taught me how to feel *with* my body, not just feel things *about* my body.

I didn't use these modalities in isolation; they wove together over time. Sometimes a session would be rooted in IFS, with somatic tracking layered in. Sometimes I'd be in a medicine state with both PSIP and parts work happening simultaneously. What mattered most wasn't the specific modality—it was the *relationship* between these tools, my therapists, and my system. That's where the healing happened.

A NOTE ON KETAMINE

This book includes personal accounts of therapeutic ketamine use as part of my healing journey. I share these experiences not as medical advice, but as reflections from my own process within legal, professionally guided settings. I do not use ketamine lightly or recreationally.

Ketamine is a powerful medicine, but it is not without risks. Its misuse, especially outside of clinical supervision, can be dangerous and, in some cases, fatal. The death of actor Matthew Perry has brought that reality into the limelight.

If you're curious about ketamine therapy, please consult with a qualified professional. I also refer to alternative medicine journeys on occasion, all of which were done legally and under professional supervision. Setting, dosage, intention, and supervision *matter*. This book is not an endorsement or a warning. It is simply the truth about the role that ketamine and other medicines have played in my healing journey.

INTRODUCTION

A gentle nudge from within, calling me toward something deeper, even when I didn't yet understand what it was.

The first song I share in this book reflects a truth I sensed long before I ever began this formal healing journey. Even before I knew what I was looking for, something inside me was calling—nudging me to go deeper, to question more, to reach toward something beyond the numbed-out life I was surviving in. There was no singular moment of clarity, but rather a slow awakening—until eventually, I reached a point of no return: a diagnosis of MS. I could no longer pretend not to hear that inner call.

Three years ago, I walked into my current therapist's office hopeful. Not hopeful that therapy would "work," but rather I was hopeful that the psychedelics would allow me to go deeper and do the work for me. I didn't just carry hope into Ashley's office that morning. I also carried a fantasy that a few ketamine sessions would somehow magically "fix" me, even though I didn't have a clue what needed fixing. I would later learn this was an example of a "salvation fantasy" after reading the book *cPTSD: From Surviving to Thriving* by Pete Walker. I didn't yet know the depth of what was living underneath my skin, but I quickly learned that there was enough unprocessed emotional baggage lurking below the surface that this was not going to be quick *or* easy.

Since that first session, Ashley and I have explored my inner world using a blend of modalities: both with and without psychedelics. While each of these has offered something meaningful on its own, what's truly unfolded is an organic integration of them all into something uniquely powerful for me.

Together we've opened doors into spaces I never thought I would access. We even opened doors to spaces I didn't know existed. And I learned how to feel those spaces. Healing begins in the feeling. But it has also come with a price tag. It has been incredibly painful at times. There is real pain underneath all of the survival tactics. It turns out I can't get out of survival mode without feeling the things that created the need for survival. There is paradoxical beauty in that pain. The more I hurt, the more I know I am healing.

Among all the tools in therapy, IFS has emerged as the central thread of my healing. What had previously felt like chaos wasn't just noise—it was a cacophony of distinct voices I'd never learned to hear separately. The angry voice that berated me for every mistake. The hopeful voice that kept me searching for something more. The scared voice that almost inaudibly whispered I wasn't safe. I didn't know yet that these weren't just thoughts; they were actually parts of me, each with their own story. Some with wounds, some with jobs. All fiercely loyal to keeping me safe.

Over time, I began to understand my internal landscape with remarkable depth. Eventually, I started to lead the system with compassion. Not all the time, mind you. I still have plenty of moments where the old familiar chaos reigns. But healing isn't linear, nor is it finite. There are baby steps, retreats, giant leaps forward, spirals, and nosedives followed by desperate rescue missions. There are moments of "I'm really getting this" and moments of "I haven't changed at all." But ALL of the moments have meaning along the way.

The combination of IFS with psychedelic therapy, especially ketamine, has allowed my parts to come to life in vivid ways.

Sometimes I have direct conversations with parts that are far more clear than during regular (non-medicine) therapy sessions. At other times, I *become* a part. I assume the energy, focus, and even speech patterns of a distinct part. One of the clearest examples is a Manager part I call the Comedian, who often shows up in ketamine sessions by cracking jokes or laughing uncontrollably through moments of discomfort. In non-medicine sessions, I can *observe* the Comedian. In medicine sessions, I *am* the Comedian. These immersive experiences have, over time, built trust. Trust in the process and trust in myself.

While ketamine has helped me build momentum and access internal material, it is not necessary. IFS alone is a powerful healing tool. It just takes longer to "get there."

When I first started IFS, I didn't trust it. I would close my eyes and try to connect with a part, but the voice I heard often triggered skepticism. (Early on I didn't recognize that skepticism as a distinct part, but I would come to know my

Skeptic very well in later medicine sessions when abuse started surfacing.)

I wondered, "Am I just saying what I think I'm supposed to say?" My Skeptic part would view any messages received with disbelief that it was really some part speaking. Rather, it would blame another part, my Analyzer (a part that thinks through and analyzes everything), for making something up to fill in gaps. It took time, and some quieting of the Skeptic, to realize that the voices I heard weren't fiction. They weren't the overactive thinker making up what might make sense. They were parts of me that had always been there, finally getting airtime.

At first, things were simple. I could identify singular parts like my Inner Critic or the Analyzer. But quickly, my system revealed its complexity. I'd begin with one part and minutes later find myself five parts removed, lost in a swarm of voices. It felt like walking into a crowded family reunion where everyone was talking at once. Overwhelmed, I backed away from trying to do the work on my own.

Eventually, I began to understand that while each part is distinct, many share similar roles and needs. Manager parts, for example, often speak the same language. Exiles share another. Once I started tuning into those patterns, I no longer needed to identify each part by name. I just needed to understand what kind of energy I was feeling. That simplified things again.

But the simplicity didn't last. As I began building relationships with more parts, especially Exiles, the conversations became layered. Many parts would speak at once. Richard Schwartz describes Self as the undamaged, natural core of your being. The goal of IFS is to bring Self into the leadership role. The more I was able to access my Self and let it lead, the more I was able to hold the complexity. With growing Self energy and experience, I no longer felt overwhelmed. I was learning to hold the system and at times lead it, not just listen to it.

Initially, I struggled to connect with my parts outside of therapy. I tried guided meditations, journaling, and silent inquiries, but nothing felt natural. It wasn't until I started writing *to* my parts that something clicked. The words began to flow. And eventually, I didn't just write the conversation. I started *hearing* them before the pen hit the page. Now writing is simply the way I record the dialogues already happening inside.

Each letter in this book is a snapshot—a moment of presence between my Self and the parts that shape me. They are not polished essays. Some were scribbled on the couch next to my dog. Some were written at 3:00 a.m. when I couldn't sleep. Some came in the middle of a chaotic day. These aren't sequenced in a formal arc, but they follow the rhythm of healing: nonlinear, messy, and alive.

You'll meet my Managers, who are some of the fiercest you'll ever encounter. You'll meet my wounded Exiles. You'll meet Firefighters, including one driven by suicidal energy. Most of all, you'll meet my Self—the steady presence that has learned to lead this inner family.

I want to offer one reassurance before you begin: if you're doing IFS and feel like it's not working, or your experience doesn't look like mine, don't worry. In the early days, I felt just as lost. Sometimes it felt too simple. Sometimes it felt far too complex. What I've learned is that the fluctuations aren't in the model. They're in us. The model stays steady. We change as we discover ourselves. And no matter where you are in the process, you are not behind. You're right on time.

IFS is not just a framework. It's a way of being with ourselves. It's not about labeling or fixing. It is about relating. These letters reflect that journey.

MEET THE CHARACTERS: MY PARTS

An invitation to face the inner battle of competing voices and step into authenticity.

The Managers try to prevent pain by keeping things orderly, controlled, or emotionally distant.

The Historian keeps a record of everything that's ever happened, often reminding me how things went in the past. It tries to keep me safe by keeping me in the familiar—because the unknown is always riskier.

The Skeptic questions everything. Especially the uncomfortable experiences that arise in medicine sessions. If it's not real, it can't hurt. That's how it protects me.

The Inner Critic points out every flaw and shortcoming. It believes that if I feel ashamed enough in advance, I'll avoid situations that could expose me or make me vulnerable.

The Analyzer keeps me out of the body and in the head by overthinking and rationalizing everything. It protects me from going into hurting places by distracting me with thoughts.

The Comedian covers pain with punchlines. Keeps things light when the weight gets too heavy.

The Guardian is a Self-like part that has been leading the search for true Self for a long time. Sometimes I wonder if she's who I was before the damage occurred.

The Firefighters jump in fast when emotions become overwhelming. Their goal is immediate relief—at any cost.

The Food Firefighter uses food (often in addictive ways) to soothe, numb, or push down the pain. Especially when other parts are screaming.

The Suicide Firefighter offers the ultimate escape when the pain feels unbearable. It's not trying to kill me—it's trying to *end suffering* the only way it knows how.

The Exiles are the parts that carry the deepest wounds—the ones that were hidden away long ago because they were too painful, too raw, or too "much."

The Chest Exile is an infant-aged part that lives in my chest and carries the memory of being suffocated. Physical abuse. No breath. No safety.

The Gut Exile is a very young part (maybe age two) that lives in my gut. She holds a heavy burden of trauma—possibly sexual. Her voice is muffled, but her pain is loud.

The Tender One is a young, gentle part who carries the weight of emotional neglect and shame. She is pure, loving, and soft—the part I've fought the hardest to protect.

This is not an exhaustive list of my parts. I have many more. These, however, are the most prominent and are the main players described throughout the book. I will also say that the focus of this book isn't what happened to me. I only remember fragmented pieces of that. Ultimately, what happened is far less important than how what happened shaped me and how I am learning to relate to myself and my parts. That is the focus of this book.

PART I

The Fall and
The Unseen Wound

CHAPTER ONE

Running On Empty

THE ULTIMATE HIGH

"Unstoppable"
—Sia

*An anthem of power and determination —
the high of believing I could conquer anything.*

November 24, 2019

It's a crisp Arizona morning in November. The sun is just peek-ing over the horizon. I am standing in my wetsuit, surrounded by roughly 2,000 other athletes. I have spent the last twelve months training for this moment, one that I have been dreaming about for years. I am finally at the starting line of Ironman Arizona.

For those unfamiliar, an Ironman is a triathlon consisting of a 2.4-mile swim, a 112-mile bike ride, and a 26.2-mile run, with a time limit of under 17 hours to complete it. My heart is racing. I have no idea what the next 17 hours will bring.

With each wave of athletes who enters the water, I inch my way closer to the swim start line. Finally, it's my turn and I dive into the 63-degree water. The cold shocks me, and I can't catch my breath. But stroke by stroke and breath by breath I make my way through 2.4 miles of frigid lake water to the swim out. Fighting cramps in my legs, I strip off the wetsuit, and begin the short jog to transition.

Hypothermic from the cold water, I am disoriented. I quickly switch into bike gear, but I need help from transition volunteers. For a brief moment, I'm not sure where I am. And I am unsure if I will be able to continue. But despite the first set-back of the day, I manage to get on my bike and head out for the 112-mile ride through the streets and rural roads of Tempe, Arizona. I am still on my goal pace.

With each of three loops on the bike, I pass by a group of friends who traveled to Tempe to cheer me on. They are loud and joyful, and with each pass lift my spirits as the grind of the day starts to overcome me. Mile by mile, cramp by cramp, and with the winds fighting against me, I next push through to mile 17 of the run before a hard cutoff ends my night early. I turn my timing chip in to race officials, then I shift my attention to my friends and allow them to support me. We hug. We cry. I hug my coach, Jess. Nearly sixteen hours after entering the water, I am done. Exhausted and in pain, I sit and reflect on the day. An older version of me would have been devastated, angry even, about not finishing. But this version of me is feeling joyful. I am celebrating what I *did* accomplish, not ruminating on what I failed to do. I feel supported. Loved. *Worthy.*

Despite what was one of the most physically challenging things I have ever done and coming up just short, I felt a real sense of peace. I didn't leave Arizona with a medal. But I did leave with feelings of pride and of hope. I felt healthy and whole. The Ironman had given me a sense of purpose, and for the first time in a long time, I felt truly *alive.*

I thought I'd outrun the past. But as I would soon learn, I'd only temporarily evaded it.

TO THE ULTIMATE LOW

"She Used to Be Mine"
—Sarah Bareilles

A lament for the self I had lost, the one who once felt alive but had slipped away.

Four months after the race in Arizona, it all came crashing down. I didn't want to get out of bed. I had no energy, motivation, or goal. My purpose had vanished. I also had a falling out with my coach, which, for reasons that were not yet clear, was emotionally devastating.

One night in March, I went to bed feeling physically well but depressed. I woke up the next morning with tingling in both feet.

What began as post-race blues quickly evolved into something much darker. After a wide range of labs and scans, I was eventually diagnosed with Multiple Sclerosis (MS). The diagnosis stunned me. Training for the Ironman had given me a sense of control over my body and life. Less than a year after my race, a diagnosis stole that sense of agency. No amount of willpower or endurance training could outpace what was now happening to me and inside me.

My symptoms appeared in March of 2020, just as the Covid lockdowns began. I spent hours in medical clinics, MR scanners, and procedure rooms, masked and alone. I was uncertain about my health and about the world around me. I remember lying in a hospital bed in the recovery room after my spinal tap (a confirmatory test for MS), scared. I hoped it was negative, but deep down I knew. What if I *did* have MS? What did that mean? How was my life going to change? It was a lonely, surreal moment of two life-changing events colliding.

The spinal tap results did come back positive, and I was officially diagnosed with MS in September of 2020. I went through all the emotions: shock, grief, and then anger. After that, I settled into a misguided version of acceptance, first believing it was here to teach me a lesson, then becoming fixated on two things: learning the lesson and eradicating it. Living *with* it wasn't an option.

I tried lifestyle changes, mainly an autoimmune diet, which I couldn't stick to faithfully. Not only that, but food cravings returned, and I found myself eating pizza and ice cream late at night. The weight followed. I thought I had moved beyond this, as I hadn't had cravings since long before my Ironman, but clearly I hadn't.

I tried countless different supplements that I gave up on weeks before they even had a chance to work. I invested in numerous alternative therapies, such as red light therapy. I floated from one approach to another, grasping for anything that might stick, but nothing seemed to help.

Then I picked up a book, *When the Body Says No* by Gabor Maté, MD, which is about the link between chronic illness and emotion.

I underlined this sentence and read it again and again:

Repression—dissociating emotions from awareness and relegating them to the unconscious realm—disorganizes and confuses our physiological defenses so that in some people these defenses go awry, becoming the destroyers of health rather than its protectors.

I became convinced that the MS was connected to repressed emotion, and I set out to uncover mine—without a clue about what was in there. I figured there had to be something. After all, I had cycled into depression numerous times in life, most recently right before the onset of symptoms.

I'd been a casual student of Joe Dispenza before the MS diagnosis, but after it, I dove into his meditation work more deeply with the intention of accessing these repressed emotions. I even attended several of his week-long meditation workshops. Afterward, I'd have a positive outlook for a brief period, but nothing changed.

Breathwork and a variety of other techniques did not help either. I grew frustrated and started blaming myself for being a failure. Now I understand I had parts that were frustrated, and my Inner Critic blamed me for not doing it right.

Over time, as I struggled with the MS and my attempt to heal it, I was also devoting more of my time and energy to caring for my aging parents, both of whom were morbidly obese and chair-bound. As their health steadily declined, their needs exponentially grew, placing an overwhelming demand on my time, energy, and finances.

I was working full time in a job I didn't really care for. I am a radiologist, and at the time I was working from home at night. It was isolating and lonely.

In the evenings, I sat for hours before my only companion—a glowing computer screen—and observed the quiet hum of a world I no longer felt a part of.

Looking back, I can see a pattern clearly:

1. Something inside me gets excited and driven and pushes me to set an impossible goal (Ironman)

2. The goal-oriented parts take charge, and life feels worthwhile.

3. Parts that carry despair take over, and I spiral into depression and self-destruction.

It was as if different versions of me were taking turns at the wheel, each with their own agenda, none of them talking to each other.

ON THE BRINK

"Rock Bottom"
—*Citizen Soldier*

The sound of despair: when inner demons are relentless and hope feels far away.

April 2022

Pulling into the parking lot of my Pilates appointment, my cell phone rings. "Dad" pops up on the screen. Before I even answer, my body tenses up and I start to get angry. As I hit the green button on the phone, I think, "What now?"

"My oxygen isn't working, Can you come home?"

My anger grows as I cancel my appointment and drive back to my parents' house. I walk in the door, fuming at how once again their needs are taking precedence over my own. I barely speak to my mom, who is sitting in her usual chair in the living room, as I pass by to my dad's bedroom.

"It seems fixed now," he says.

That is the final straw.

I start yelling.

He interrupts me: "I'm sorry I'm such a burden. I wish I could just die."

Without thinking, and with my angry voice, I yell back, "Trust me, Dad, if you didn't need me, I would blow my brains out right now."

My stomach drops. I feel sick.

That was a horrifying exchange with my dad. I couldn't believe what I said to him. It wasn't me. Afterward, the guilt hit hard. But it was also a loud wake-up call that things had escalated far beyond my ability to cope.

I had been researching psychedelic therapy as a possible way to access my elusive emotional debris that I believed was fueling my illness. But now, in addition to seeking healing for the MS, I needed a way to survive. The depression had spiraled into a full-on life crisis. I needed help.

In March of 2022, just before the blowup with my dad, I wrote a journal entry titled "Anger Unleashed." I listed nine things I was angry about, including my parents, my brother, the MS, and the world. Four of the nine entries started the same way: "I am angry at myself for . . ." followed by an explanation for my anger.

The last one, however, had the biggest impact of all. It simply said:

"I am angry at myself for WHO I AM."

If there was ever a time to seek therapy, this was it.

THE TURNING POINT

"Be Slow"
—Harrison Storm

*A reminder to breathe, to slow down,
to let healing come in its own time.*

The grief.

The anger.

The physical pain.

The loss of control.

I was spiraling, and it was time to slow down and breathe. I reached out to a friend. She recommended a local therapist who was offering a legal and accessible form of psychedelic therapy. Apprehensive, I dialed Ashley's office.

Asking for help would turn out to be one of the greatest decisions I have ever made.

CHAPTER TWO

The Moment Everything Changed

"Watershed"
—Indigo Girls

*The feeling of standing at a crossroads,
knowing indecision weighs heavy
and change is inevitable.*

THE NEW THERAPIST

"A Safe Place to Land"
—Sarah Bareilles and John Legend

A promise of support: someone will catch you when you can't carry yourself anymore.

July 2022

I take a sip of my coffee. Sitting in a not-so-comfortable chair in the waiting room at Ashley's office, I look around. Contemporary furniture. A bookcase filled with books on a variety of topics, some of which I have in my own library.

I think back to prior experiences with therapy and how uncomfortable I was. The exposure, the probing questions, the discomfort with sitting in a room with a stranger, all nagging at me. This time feels different, though, because I won't have to talk much. I am here to do ketamine and let the drug do the work.

I take another sip of coffee and flip through a picture book on IFS and Parts sitting on the coffee table. Finally, Ashley opens the door and invites me into her office. I feel self-conscious; my heart is racing. I walk in and sit on her tan leather couch. I take a deep breath, and she asks me what brings me in. Where do I even start? I audibly exhale.

There is so much to say. I take a another deep breath and start talking. I tell her about the MS, my parents, my job, the post-Ironman emptiness, and how I hope ketamine will some-how "fix" the things I can't seem to reach.

I don't have any big trauma in my past. Most people I have read about who healed from chronic illness had stories of abuse. I have none. Yeah, I've been overweight my entire life, but I was bullied only a little. I was popular in school. I had lots of friends. My parents loved me and each other. There was no addiction in my family. Zero trauma.

As far as I could recall, I had a happy childhood, and I was a successful adult, although I admittedly struggled with depression at times. I attributed that to situational stressors like caring for aging parents and my job, as well as poor body image because of my weight.

I had overcome a lot of that, though, through personal work over the years. I didn't see any reason why I would have enough stored emotion inside to cause an illness such as MS. I was chasing an elusive ghost. What I didn't yet understand was that trauma can hide in the absence of obvious events, buried in all the unnoticed moments that shape us quietly.

I told Ashley a lot of things that first day—but not once did I talk about how I felt. I couldn't. I wasn't feeling, and I was so numb I didn't even know I wasn't feeling. Looking back I see it clearly, although at the time it didn't register as abnormal.

When I finished talking, Ashley asked a few questions with a quiet confidence. She asked me more about my mom. She asked more about my best friend Michelle. She was seeing patterns in my relationships that I couldn't.

I also think she noticed more in my energy and how guarded I was than she got from what I had shared. She could see right through the stories I was telling and saw the wounds I had been trying, and failing, to access for so long. She didn't know the exact shape of them, but she knew they were there. I had not officially met my parts yet, but that day, Ashley did. And perhaps most importantly, she recognized that the biggest wound of all was the absence of an obvious one.

THE NEW LENS

"Easy On Me"
—Adele

A plea for compassion for the child-self who never had the chance to grow freely.

Ashley introduced me to the concepts of emotional neglect and complex PTSD (cPTSD). She suggested a couple of books, and just like that, a new lens began to form. I listened to the audiobook *Running on Empty* by Jonice Webb, PhD, on a long solo road trip to Denver. If you've ever traveled it, you know that I-70 through Western Kansas and Eastern Colorado is the perfect place to queue up an audiobook.

The book is about emotional neglect: what it is, what it looks like in people who suffer from it, and how to begin healing from it. I was captivated by every word. It felt like I was listening to someone describe, in intimate detail, my inner world in a way I never could. Jonice gave a voice to the quiet ill ease I had carried my entire life. For the first time, I had a blueprint of the internal wiring I always knew was different but never could quite name or describe. This book was me.

It was so profound, I had to stop driving several times to journal. As I listened, there were waves of thoughts and emotions bubbling up. Mostly I felt a sense of relief that there was something real underneath my lifelong ache. I was finally understood. THIS WAS IT!! The ghost I had been chasing all this time had a name: emotional neglect. I now knew that I didn't lack significant trauma, but rather my trauma was an insidious absence. It was trauma in disguise.

By the end of the introduction of the book, I was already recognizing myself in her words.

> *Many fine, high-functioning, capable people secretly feel unfulfilled or disconnected. "Shouldn't I be happier?" "Why haven't I accomplished more?" "Why doesn't my life feel more meaningful?" These are questions which are often prompted by the invisible force at work. They are often asked by people who believed that they had loving, well-meaning parents and who remember their childhoods as mostly happy and healthy. So they blame themselves for whatever doesn't feel right as an adult. They don't realize they are under the influence of what they don't remember. . . . The invisible force.*
>
> —Jonice Webb, *Running on Empty*

I had asked myself those very questions many times over the years. She goes on to label this invisible force as emotional neglect and describes why it is so often missed:

It hides. It dwells in the sins of omission rather than commission; it's the white space in the family picture rather than the picture itself. It's often what was NOT said or observed or remembered from childhood, rather than what WAS said.

After answering yes to almost all of the symptoms of emotional neglect in a questionnaire provided in the book, I knew I had a severe case. That list of questions is provided in the Appendix.

That night, I emailed Ashley to share what had come up. I include it here, as it reflects the raw awareness in real time.

August 2022

Hi Ashley,
I'm listening to this audiobook on emotional neglect on my drive. First of all, I identify with all 10 "symptoms" she lays out in the book—some more than others, but it's very clear it's a severe case for me. What else came up listening to that section was how I have already worked on and grown in so many of the problematic areas described. I have become more self-aware and am better, i.e., friendships, etc. But it does drive home the belief now of what I've been up against all this time, and it increases the self-compassion some. It also increased awareness of what is still there and how, even though I have opened up more, I still feel vacant and alone. Listening to it, there were moments of pressure in my gut, squirming in my seat, and an urge or two to turn on some music instead—but a fascination and inability to turn it off...

What listening has done has named it, cemented
belief, made me more self-compassionate and more
proud of myself—and deepened the commitment to
this work. I don't know that I need to read, watch or
listen to one more resource to get it. I just need to dive
in. And I realize that I already have. Things are
happening. I know there is so much anger and grief
under the surface.
Kim

Sent from my iPhone

Relief poured over me—naming the ghost I'd been chasing for years. Finally, I was being seen, even if only by a voice in an audiobook. And as I shared it with Ashley, I could feel it. Ashley saw me too.

Things were about to shift. I was starting to feel trust, and I was finally telling the truth. I was no longer chasing shadows. I had something real to work with.

Even though I had just written that I didn't need another resource, I immediately dove into the second book Ashley recommended: *cPTSD: From Surviving to Thriving* by Pete Walker, MA, MFT. With each chapter, my awareness continued to grow.

This book introduced the concept of cPTSD and emotional flashbacks. I already understood the basics of traditional PTSD, which is universally recognized and well understood as often tied to a singular traumatic event. For example, a war veteran may be sitting safely at home and, upon hearing a loud noise, suddenly feels as if they are back on the battlefield. The stimulus is clear, and the reaction is outwardly noticeable and usually dramatic. It makes sense.

But cPTSD is different. It isn't caused by a single traumatic event, but rather by a slow accumulation of many small, ongoing wounds. Many of these, like emotional neglect, are invisible. So the flashbacks it creates are not to a specific moment but rather to an overwhelming emotional state such as shame, fear, abandonment, or worthlessness—often all at once. The triggers are often subtle and unassuming: a missed text, a look or a tone of voice, a cancellation of plans. The reaction also may be minor on the surface but raging below it. Inside, the experience is deeply familiar and just as consuming.

Unlike the battlefield flashback, emotional flashbacks are hard to recognize, even by the person having them. There is no obvious memory attached to the flashback—only a flood of feeling that hijacks the inner world. Flashing back to an emotion is much more insidious than flashing back to an event.

I recognized those deep, intense feelings as moments from the repetitive childhood trauma of neglect, and suddenly so many of my patterns made sense. I also recognized that I do, in fact, have emotion. It's not buried in some locked container waiting to be released; it's been leaking out all along in the form of flashbacks I didn't realize I was experiencing. It turns out that I did indeed have trauma and had been living in a world of emotional PTSD for years.

Until I met Ashley, I wasn't aware of this, nor was I aware of its fallout in my system. Armed with this new awareness and a fresh sense of hope, I dug in.

BREADCRUMBS

"This Is Your Life"
—Switchfoot

*A challenge to stop living on autopilot and ask:
is this really the life I want?*

At this point, after only a few sessions with Ashley and reading her recommended resources, it was as if someone had handed me a completely new lens to view my life, and suddenly, everything looked different.

Discovering emotional neglect and complex PTSD was like the revealing moment in the movie *The Sixth Sense* (spoiler alert if you haven't seen the movie) when the viewer realizes that Bruce Willis's character was dead all along. Once the plot twist is revealed, you go back and replay every scene in your mind, seeing each one very differently.

In the same way, once the hidden truth of my internal landscape came into focus, I started to see every scene in my life with new eyes. Suddenly, things that never quite made sense fell into place. And for the first time, my story (and my Self) began to feel clear. There was a real sense of relief in it, but there was also a heaviness in realizing that it took fifty years and several therapists to reach the plot twist in my story.

I had always known something was not quite right, but I prided myself on the fact that I was "normal." Sure, I had life stress and situational demands that got to me, but I was mentally wired just fine. It was a defense mechanism I would later discover was due to some of my parts working to protect me from what was underneath. But I was finally seeing that I had some massive faulty wiring behind the stoic "I'm fine" front. It was around this time that I realized this was not going to be a quick and easy fix.

Although it took me a hot minute to settle into the idea of long-term therapy, Ashley told me right up front that I was going to have to work with the things within me rather than chase them away with a few ketamine sessions.

I still remember her saying to me in the first (or maybe second) appointment, "Oh, I expect to be working with you for several years." That was *not* what I'd envisioned. Healing, yes. Years of therapy? Not so much.

Yet, here I am almost three years later, deeply entrenched in my healing with no "end" in sight, and committed to however long it might take to feel complete with the process.

I didn't have the language of emotional neglect or cPTSD before therapy. Once I learned to recognize it, I could see how alive it was and how it had shaped me. "That is just how I am" thoughts began to shift. And with the introduction of IFS, I also began to recognize how my parts were trying to communicate with me all along.

Despite not yet having conscious awareness of emotional neglect, my system already knew.

That knowing is scattered across old journals, written before I began therapy with Ashley. My parts were speaking through me, their voices buried in my words.

Several months before I walked into Ashley's office, I discovered a book, *Writing the Mind Alive: The Proprioceptive*

Method for Finding Your Authentic Voice, by Linda Metcalf and Tobin Simon. The method invited me to write from a deeper place, with candlelight, music, and prompts that asked me to stay with my language. If I wrote, "It's hard," I'd be prompted to ask, "What do I mean by 'hard'?"

I practiced this ritual for a few weeks, but it didn't help me settle. I was still living in survival mode and eventually abandoned the practice. It wasn't until much later, after beginning therapy, that I rediscovered those pages. I was stunned at what was written on them. My wounded parts, especially my Exiles, had been present all along.

What follows is an excerpt from the very first piece I wrote using that method. Themes of shame, neglect, and deep loneliness emerge with striking clarity.

3/1/22 – First Write

This is my first write. I'm excited but also anxious—though I'm often anxious.

What do I mean by anxious? Just not comfortable.

What do I mean by comfortable? I don't really know. It's something I think about, but I'm not sure I've ever actually felt it.

My arm's already tired.

I think all the time—nonstop—but when I try to reflect, my thoughts disappear.

It's like I'm scared of them. What do I mean by scared?

I'm afraid someone will see me the way I see me.

How do I see me?

A fat little girl who never felt like she fit in.

> I feel heat rise—shame.
> I remember when a chair broke under me in class in college.
> My fatness exposed. Raw.
> What do I mean by raw?
> Unprotected. Embarrassed.
> It's worse when people see pain that's tied to my shame.
> If I lost a parent, I wouldn't mind showing that pain—I'd even want people to feel sorry for me.
> I wanted nurturing.
> What do I mean by that?
> To be seen. For someone to understand I was hurting.
> But not to know why I was hurting. The truth felt too embarrassing.

Reading this now, I can feel the weight of what I didn't yet understand. At the time, I thought I was just struggling to write and to "do it right." But underneath that self-monitoring was a chorus of parts trying to speak through me.

I see the Exile who carried shame like a second skin. The one who learned that being seen in her pain was dangerous unless the pain was deemed socially acceptable. I see the part who longed for nurturing but couldn't bear to expose the reason why she needed it. And I see the part who tried so hard to stay in control by thinking her way through everything, only to find herself blank when emotions arose. Words like "nurturing" weren't words I would normally use; they were coming from parts that were just below the surface.

What strikes me most is that even though I didn't know the language of parts yet, they were already trying to reach me.

They showed up through my words, my physical sensations, and my silences. They were always there, waiting for me to listen differently.

MAYBE

"Maybe"
—From the Broadway show Annie

The Orphan and the Longing

Here is a second writing from that same time period that has just as much rich metaphor from an Exile, but you can also see a Manager peeking through in the form of numbness and freeze, describing dissociation.

3/2/22 – Write #2

I didn't think about what I would write about before.

There's so much I could cover. But what just came into my head is when I was a kid.

I remember singing in a talent show. I don't remember how old I was—grade school? Or junior high maybe.

I sang Maybe from the Broadway show Annie. I can see my younger self. I loved music even then.

Excited but nervous—will it be good?

Will they like it? What do I mean by they?

Everyone.

Drawing a blank. I'm starting to sing it now.

I was singing in the show just now, and I feel a sense of reservation.

What do I mean by reservation?

My throat pinches off, airflow stops, and things feel forced.

What do I mean by force? Not natural. Hard.

Another blank. What is up there in my head?

I feel mad a lot. Not right now, but often.

When I get mad, it's that same forced belly-like—

Like I'm going to explode.

Another blank.

I keep seeing in my mind a picture of my grade school self.

So self-conscious. I just want to be liked.

So lonely. Why can't I remember specifics about my childhood?

When I think about it I can just see my face in my grade school picture.

What do I mean by lonely?

I'm unsure/scared. Scared of my dad.

I'm going blank again.

Maybe I'm numb to it.

What do I mean by numb? Frozen.

What do I mean by frozen? Afraid to move, to make decisions, to speak up, to be seen.

I'm fat and big but want to not be noticed.

Please don't notice me.

I think I'm confused about who I am.

I think back to that little girl wishing to be different.

I chose the song "Maybe" for that talent show, which is about Annie's longing for loving parents. I didn't realize it then, but that song choice wasn't random. It was my Exile speaking through me—singing her wish into the world the only way she knew how. My exile was singing even then, as a young girl.

Looking back, there are numerous breadcrumbs that were leading me on the path inward. I see that it was never about getting my parts to speak. It was about learning how to listen.

Armed with the new awareness around emotional neglect and cPTSD, I started revisiting things from my childhood and saw a different picture than the one I had in my memory bank. Honestly, it became clear just how *little* of my childhood I actually remembered. It wasn't that I couldn't remember much. It was that the absence itself started to feel like the memory. Not being able to remember was the important thing.

I could recall a few things here or there, but I had little memory of how I *felt*. As a child, I buried emotions just like my parents had modeled. When I tried to remember hearing my mom say, "I love you" to me, I couldn't. I tried to remember a comforting moment with her holding my hand or hugging me. I couldn't. I tried to remember crying in her arms. I couldn't.

I was astonished at how little I relied on anyone to help me process anything that came my way. I had been emotionally alone my entire life, even as a young child. I knew my parents loved me. But *knowing* I was loved was entirely different than feeling it. It was the felt sense of love that had always been absent—and that absence was and is at the core of my distress, even now.

I don't say this to blame my parents. They did the very best they could, but they were also highly damaged and shut down themselves; they simply couldn't give me what they didn't have to give.

As I continued to look back, the memories I did have began to take on new meaning. I saw a little girl who wet the bed for years—well into junior high. I had always seen this experience through the external lens of embarrassment: things like not being able to attend sleepovers or go on camping trips.

But now what stood out was the silence at home with my parents. While they did take me to doctor appointments in search of a cause, they never actually talked to me about it. Not once do I remember being held, comforted, or reassured. I just remember Mom changing the bedsheets every morning, sometimes in frustration. Who could blame her? Washing and changing bedding every single day is a drag.

I knew I was doing something wrong, but rather than being met with warmth and comfort, at best I was met with quiet detachment or visible frustration. The silence said more than words ever could. I internalized all of it, not as a condition I was struggling with, but as evidence that I was bad. That silence blanketed a great deal of my childhood.

Comfort was missing in the small everyday things too. Without conversations with my parents about feelings, I learned to keep my emotions to myself.

But I wasn't just keeping them to myself; I was burying them so deep I didn't even know what emotions I was feeling. Even if I *did* know, I never learned how to express them. Neither parent taught me, and at times it may have seemed like it wasn't safe or "correct" to do so.

There is one night I remember like it was yesterday. I was

in high school, and by then I had been playing softball since I was six. I was really good and made the varsity team as a freshman. I was so excited. but I'd been plagued by persistent back pain throughout the preseason.

One week before the first game, I started having trouble sitting. The pain had become severe, and I was experiencing weird sensations in my legs. I told my mom about it after practice one night, and soon after I was in the doctor's office getting scans. The diagnosis? I had a stress fracture in my back, and just like that, after months of preseason conditioning and practices, I was out for the season.

The night I got home from the doctor, I sat in the rocking chair in the living room, devastated but numb. My mom, seated across the room on the couch, seemed indifferent to the gravity of what I might be feeling. We sat watching TV in that all-too-familiar silence.

I eventually got up and fixed myself a bowl of chili. I had already eaten dinner and wasn't hungry, but the pattern of eating to stuff down emotion was already raging by that time. As I sat down with it, the doorbell rang. Mom answered, and I was horrified to hear my coach's voice at the door. (This was well before cell phones and text messages.)

I scrambled to hide the chili so my coach wouldn't see me eating it. She wasn't a particularly warm and nurturing person. She was a "suck it up, chin up" kind of woman, and that's what her visit was: a pep talk. While it was nice to know someone was thinking about me, it wasn't what I needed.

I had no clue what I *did* need, though. I thought my chili, which I went back to eating after my coach left, was all I needed.

When this memory came up during a psilocybin journey

in July 2023, I found myself weeping deep, guttural tears. Real emotion was surfacing around it. I was shocked by the intensity of the emotion and confused about why this memory would even surface. During integration, I shared my confusion with the guide. "It isn't like it's that big of a deal. I don't know why I'm crying so much about it," I told her.

"Was softball your identity?" she asked. And then it hit. Yes. Yes, it was. Not being able to play was a deep rupture in my very core.

But what struck me the most was this: Not only was there a complete lack of nurturing and support during what turned out to be a core emotional wound, but I was so detached from my own feelings that I didn't even know I needed those things and wasn't getting them.

One of the features of emotional neglect is a fleeting and false sense of self. I was never grounded in my own Self energy but attached to things, like softball or Ironman. My high school back injury was neither the first nor the last time my false sense of self would be ripped away. Years later, the MS would do something eerily similar.

Once again, a false sense of self (fitness and health freak) was stripped away, and I found myself deep in a new one: chronic illness/MS. The further I got down the road of healing the MS, the more I realized that this journey wasn't about fixing the illness or getting back to who I was before the MS.

It was about discovering who I really am underneath all the coping and survival.

DISSOLVING THE
SALVATION FANTASY

"Bitter Ender"
—Mary Chapin Carpenter

The realization that magical thinking doesn't bring healing — only honesty does.

I now knew I wasn't feeling my emotions and had plenty of reason for stored ones.

The breakthroughs in self-awareness were both a blessing and a curse.

My entire life up to that point felt very fake and superficial. I wasn't actually *living* it; I was hidden behind all sorts of walls and coping mechanisms that were maladaptive at best and destructive at worst. (Stuffing my feelings down with food being one of the most destructive.)

At the same time, there was a deep sense of relief that I finally understood this. And with that understanding came a glimmer of hope. Hope that the loneliness and depression that had silently plagued me throughout life might actually shift. I was ready, and willing, to roll up my sleeves and do the hard work with Ashley.

The salvation fantasy had dissolved, not in disappointment, but in the quiet realization that healing wasn't magic. It was relationship. It was presence. And it had already begun.

I inherently knew I was about to move toward my pain rather than avoiding it like I had so masterfully done in the past.

In an early journal writing, I wrote:

Sept. 2022

If I am going to improve—mentally, emotionally, physically, and spiritually—I need to get uncomfortable. I need to be curious about the discomfort rather than run from it or fear it.

I also had a tiny glimpse of Self energy as I continued to write:

The key is to have faith that the discomfort won't last forever. The key is to remember that ultimately, there is no problem. Only evolution. As long as I keep evolving, I am ok. I have had so many experiences— and I like new ones. The one wild frontier—the new experience that awaits me now—is love.

This was a watershed moment. For so long, I had stood at the fork in the road, agonizing under the weight of not knowing why I felt the way I did. But now, the agony had a name. And with that clarity, I chose a path—not the one that led back to comfort, but the one that pointed toward the unknown. Toward healing.

Toward home.

Toward love.

PART II

Meeting the Inner World

CHAPTER THREE

Internal Wars—Conflicting Parts

THE INNER CRITIC

"Monsters"
—*Shinedown*

*A vivid portrait of the critic inside,
like a monster trained to wound.*

One of the most challenging aspects of parts work is how often parts act in direct opposition. Just picture the Inner Critic shouting, "Put that cupcake down because you're fat enough as it is!" At the same time, there's an emotional fire that a firefighter is trying desperately to put out with that cupcake.

Both parts are doing what they think is in my best interest. Both parts, loyal and hardworking, are simply trying to protect me the only way they know how. This is just one example of a much broader and familiar pattern.

Initially, the parts felt fragmented, and working with them in isolation highlighted this internal tug-of-war below the surface. Talk about tension! When you have several of these internal battles all going on at once, or a trigger activates a five-alarm response from a firefighter to numb the pain, the anxiety soars like flames on a dry hillside. Especially when the firefighter engages in behavior the Inner Critic disapproves of, like eating junk food.

Even if you're not familiar with IFS, I'm sure you are familiar with the inner critic. We all have one—and I had been familiar with mine long before IFS therapy. When I was working with my triathlon coach Jess, I called my Inner Critic "Lazy Lu," because it always told me how lazy I was. Even then, I was working with parts. I just didn't have the language for it.

I have a very strong critic, which I came to learn is a hallmark feature of cPTSD. In *cPTSD: From Surviving to Thriving,* author Pete Walker talks about taming the inner critic as one of the first steps in recovery.

Some of my earliest parts work centered on my Inner Critic. This led to my first attempt at writing a letter to a part:

Aug. 19, 2022

To my Bully part (My Critic):

I see you. All the input about being lazy, my weight, my appearance, and my achievements was simply an effort to help me feel needed, wanted, and loved. And for many years, it helped me feel wanted and loved. It made me feel worthwhile when I actually listened to you and lost weight or accomplished a big goal. You provided the motivation to do things that created a sense of self-worth that I couldn't muster without you. I am thankful that you have been there. You have done an amazing job. For the longest time, it was when I listened to you that I felt my best. It's when I ignored your warnings and comments that I felt sad and lonely. Now though, I am stronger, and I realize that I am loved just as I am. I am worthy of love just as I am, and I am learning to feel that love without the need to have to change or accomplish anything. You can rest now. I don't want you to go away entirely—there are some things I want to accomplish, not because I need to but because I want *to. And I will need you to help me stay focused; however, there is no need to be harsh or shout anymore. I love you, and I am grateful for you. You don't have to work so hard anymore.*

CONFLICTING VOICES – INTERNAL CHAOS

"Schizophrenic Conversations"
—Staind

The chaos of battling inner voices, colliding inside one mind.

While I was all-too-familiar with my inner critic, IFS was helping me understand that if I wanted to get to the root of my self-sabotaging behaviors, I needed to look further than just my Inner Critic. At the same time I wrote that first letter, I did a short parts meditation where I had this realization:

Aug. 19, 2022 – email to Ashley

What came up is that the bully needs to step away and the self-nurturing part needs to grow much stronger. I think it is as much about teaching a part how to nurture and love as it is about having the bully back away.

What I didn't quite realize yet was that it wasn't about teaching a single part to love and telling another part to back off; it was about bringing Self energy to the table with love and nurturing for *all* of my parts—including my Inner Critic and the Food Firefighter.

Before I was aware of parts, it was just all me and the loud chaos of my incessant thoughts. But the ketamine helped slow those thoughts down and separate them to where I understood that all the noise was just my many parts all clamoring for my attention. Right after my first ketamine session, I wrote in my post-session notes:

Aug. 26, 2022

There was a lot about the "conversations" in my head. I have a lot of very active parts, and it's loud. And now it's almost as if they are aware I'm paying attention and are fighting for position.

It took over a year of regular ketamine sessions, and a lot of work in between with Ashley, to break things down into individual parts, but over time I was able to hear distinct parts and their voices through the noise. Even now, three years in, I am still meeting new distinct parts in my system.

SELF: THE INNER MEDIATOR

"I Am Light"
—India Arie

*A reminder of the Self beyond trauma —
whole, clear, unbroken.*

As I got further into my experience working with my parts and with ketamine, I was better able to navigate "multi-part" conversations, or "family meetings," where I would introduce parts to each other and make them aware of the internal conflict. In this series of internal dialogues, I invited all the major players to speak—from the Exile in despair to the parts that freeze me in fear. What followed is a kind of council meeting inside my system, where I began to mediate the parts with compassion and curiosity.

The first letter is insightful into the energy behind my Inner Critic. I shared this letter with Ashley in her office at the beginning of a session. "I can see how much energy is in your critic right now," she replied.

Conversation with my Inner Critic, Part I

Hi Kim,

I notice you have let yourself go lately. You have gained weight. You don't exercise, and you have no discipline with eating. You sit around and watch TV way too much. You should be doing something productive. You used to be so much more productive —what has happened to you? I know you want love, but you will never get it at this rate. No one will want you. I know you are trying to get better, but you are not doing enough. It's not working because you aren't committed to it. You should be meditating more. You should be journaling more. More, more, more! Nothing you do ever quite really rises to the level it needs to be. You just think you are smart, but who are you kidding? You need to study more. Know more. In fact, you need to KNOW IT ALL before you can rest. That isn't too much to ask. I am only pushing you because I love you, even though it might seem like deep down I hate you. I can't let you slide. You need to lose weight to be worthwhile. You need to be accomplishing great things to be worthwhile.

Hi critic,

Thank you so much for telling me all of that. I am so sorry you feel that I have really let myself go. I can sense how much fear there is in your voice. You are so afraid of me being lonely and feeling worthless that you have to work so tirelessly and endlessly to protect me. I do not think you hate me. In fact, I know you love me more than your words even say. You are doing a job that was forced on you a long time ago, and if I had to guess, I would say that you don't even like your job. I completely understand why you do it, though.

For a long time I really believed all of the things you were saying. But now, I have discovered that there is another truth. While the motive is so pure and loving, the content of what you say is damaging. It is hurtful but, more importantly, actually feeds the very inaction that you are so afraid of. It shuts me down more often than it motivates me these days. Maybe in time you will understand that the weight gain is actually the result of a sister that uses food to provide the same kind of protection you do, just in a different manner.

You will see that I AM worthwhile just for who I am, and no amount of work or no single accomplishment is going to be necessary to feel that worth. I am not asking you to go away. But I am asking that you take a moment to study the things I am doing and ponder if what you are saying to me is true. I think you will find that it is not. I WANT you to stick around. A good dose of motivation is not a bad thing, because I DO want to accomplish things. I DO want to be fit and active. I DO want to find love. I want to do a lot of things, but not because I need to do them to feel worthy. I just want to do them. And I could use a partner that keeps me focused and committed to whatever goal I might set or project I may tackle. But over time, you will discover that I get further with love than criticism. And your language and tone will change. Don't be alarmed. That is just you feeling worth and love too. I'll meet you there.

Notice there is slightly more compassion and understanding toward my Critic than in my first letter.

Shortly after, I went to my self-sabotage parts and asked them why I have such a sense of hopelessness around self-care. Here is an excerpt from that letter:

. . . That hopelessness seems to show up in many ways. Lack of self-care. Lack of purpose. Lack of passion. Self-defeating thoughts around change. Self-sabotaging behaviors such as eating inflammatory food. These are all things that I would rather do differently—and I also would like to get the inner critic some relief and off YOUR and my backs.

I want to hear from all of you. I want to clear the air around this. Because I want to LIVE. But I want to bring you along with me. We have to come to an understanding. I want to know what you are afraid of. I want to know what you need. I want to know how we change things—together.

Hi Kim:
This is your Exile(s). There is a deep sense of hopelessness that comes from being abused and unable to do anything about it.

It is safer to stay still and allow whatever happens to happen because there is pain and fatigue with trying to fight it. Currently there is little aversion to death, as that might be preferable to the anguish we feel all of the time.

Hi Kim:
Historian here. I am one of your managers. I am the voice that says things have always been this way and they always will. I just keep records—all kinds of records. There are familial records. Everyone in your family is obese and unhealthy. Look—you even tried to do an Ironman to change, but here you are. Right back where things started.

I also keep records of how you treat yourself. Do

you think you can change unhealthy habits? Don't think so quick. You have ALWAYS been one for sweets.

You are better off accepting things the way they are. It's safer.

Hi Kim:

Food Firefighter here. Yes, I am the one that is responsible for putting out the pain fires that erupt.

I don't hide in the shadows or try to limit my profile. I simply just act swiftly whenever I smell smoke. I don't even wait for fires anymore. I have been around long enough to know that even a whiff of smoke is dangerous, and I have a very good nose. I jump into action the only way I know how. I distract you with food.

Hi Kim:

Guardian here. I must admit that of all parts, I am probably the last one you would expect to be part of the problem. But I really thought with the Ironman you had discovered passion and purpose that you had been seeking. So imagine my surprise when MS showed up and everything changed. I was just so stunned and dismayed that even I lost hope. What good did all of my efforts do?

Hi Kim:

I am a part that is very insidious in some ways in that you aren't really that aware of me as a distinct part, but I am very prominent in my effect on you. I was born in a time when movement equaled harm. I see the world that way still. I need to stay still for your safety.

The best way I know how is to freeze you out of making decisions and acting on them because decisions equal movement. And one wrong movement could be deadly.

My response:
Hi guys. I really appreciate your willingness to share your feelings on this. I have been listening intently. Each voice is valid and welcome. I would like to share a few things:

To my exiled parts:
I have sat with you a few times now, and I do see the hopelessness. And I can't say enough how sorry I am that that happened to you. And I am even more sorry that you were abandoned through it. I hope you can feel my presence and love growing stronger each time we talk. I am not leaving you. Let that be a seed to plant a spark of hope in the darkness you have been consumed by all these years. It is hope that is going to rescue you; I am only the loving messenger.

To my Historian:
History has not been kind in more ways than one. Yes, there is a genetic/familial track record.

Yes, there is a heavily damaged personal past filled with many examples one could point to to make the argument things will never change.

Yes, there have been many instances of behavior that were all captured by my mirror.

But I would like to draw your attention to the fact that records can always be broken. Things can change—and are already changing. Rather than stay focused on the past, look gently to the here and now, and you will notice some changes already happening that do not align with the past.

To fear and overwhelm:
I will address you two together since you often show up hand in hand. I understand you feel you need to keep me immobile. I have been working with the Exiles, and I can completely understand where you are coming from. The need to be immobile for safety was very real for quite a while. Back then, movement meant imminent danger, maybe even death.

But it is you who doesn't realize that the safer choice is to move forward into better health and happiness. We no longer live in the past. I want you to see that you don't have to work so hard anymore. You can rest, knowing that movement is not danger; it is freedom.

To my oldest and most loyal part, the Food Firefighter:
We go way back. I have known you longer than any other part, I think. I just didn't understand you. Now, I do. And with that understanding comes an immense amount of respect and gratitude. I also now have so much compassion for you, because I see how hard you have worked over the years.

You started out having to put out a few fires here and there dating all the way back to when I had colic all those years ago. But now, you never get to rest. It is constant. I know you mean well. Honestly, your actions quite often do bring me comfort and sometimes even pleasure. And I don't want you to go away because I like comfort and pleasure, but only in moderation.

I am now resilient enough to survive discomfort. Sure there is smoke, but the smoke serves to direct my attention to what needs understanding, compassion, and love. Without the smoke, I cannot effectively tend to myself. I can't guarantee that on occasion some smoke might turn into a fire, but I promise I will let you step in before it is a raging four-alarm event. I just need you to give me a little space.

Lastly, to my trusted Guardian:
You have done so well in my absence all this time. Do not hang your head in dismay. You have not failed me. On the contrary, without your loyalty and effort, I would not be here now. It is YOU that stayed curious. It is YOU who kept trying in the face of disappointment and defeat. It is YOU that kept the engine running when the energy was on empty. It is YOU who organized my search party and saw it through despite the despair that you might never find me, and it is YOU who kept the light burning in the darkest of times. That light is what guided me home. You have nothing to be ashamed of and everything to be proud of. Without you, none of this would have been possible, and as we continue to move forward, I absolutely need you to stay next to me.

As I was writing to my parts, shame interrupted.

Shame here:
Sorry to interrupt you, but I want to remind you I am still here. I live inside your exiles but am just a burden

to them. You are, after all, unlovable. I am here to protect that memory. I attach myself to the very core of who you are and like to hide because keeping you fat, unhealthy, and unhappy with yourself is self-preservation. I hide in the shadows and corrupt some of your parts to guide your behaviors, becoming louder when you are closer to breaking free from my grip. You cannot escape me. I reach far and wide and while I live in your exiles' wounds, I am like an infection that has spread to every part of you.

To shame:
I have no compassion for you. I have immeasurable compassion for my exiles and my other parts, but you deny me access to them. You deny me access to myself. And you deny me access to others. You have no place here. You have been feeding off our energy long enough. My parts do not see you, but I do. You say I cannot escape you, but I can, and I will. All it takes is to shine a light upon you, and you will no longer be able to feed. Without my parts as a carrier, you will cease to exist in my system. I may not be rid of you entirely just yet, but I can tell you are concerned. The light is coming.

I want to say one final word to the group:
I love you all. And I always will. I am here now, and you can rest in me. It is time for the struggle—the constant effort—to give way to ease and rest. It is time for the shame to be lifted and give way to a renewed sense of self. It is time for the darkness and pain to give way to light and love. Is time for the loneliness of abandonment to give way to union with

me and with each other. It is time for the past to give way to a different future together.

As I listened to all the voices in my system—the Exile's hopelessness, the Historian's grim records, the Food Firefighter's desperate urgency, and the parts that freeze me in fear or overwhelm me—I began to understand something I hadn't fully seen before.

My Critic wasn't the enemy. It was scared. Terrified, even.

It had been trying so hard, in its own way, to keep me alive. And while its tactics often hurt more than helped, its loyalty was unmatched.

For so long, I had seen my Inner Critic as the villain. But now, through the eyes of Self, I could see that it, too, had been acting out of protection; it didn't trust that anyone else knew how to steer the ship. And I could also see just how committed my other parts were to their roles. There is no wrong side. All of my parts need love and understanding. That is the mediation.

It was time to respond—not with resistance or dismissal—and not to shut them down, but to invite them into a different kind of relationship. One built not on fear and control, but on trust and care.

I'm still navigating this internal conflict—it's a battle for the ages. But each time I turn toward my parts, I soften them a little more, make more room for Self, and move a little closer to peace. I'm learning that grace brings healing.

I am more and more light each day.

CHAPTER FOUR

From Thinking to Feeling

PAIN MANAGEMENT: FLOATING AND THINKING

"Breathe Me"

—Sia

*A desperate prayer for help,
for someone to see and hold me.*

When Ashley first suggested I might be dissociating, I was confused—I didn't know the term. I didn't have loss of time or dramatic blackouts. Turns out, though, I was chronically dissociated, and I didn't even know it—because it felt normal. I'd been living from the neck up for years, maybe decades. My system had adapted beautifully: stay in the head and avoid the minefield of sensation below. I could function, even thrive. But I was existing in a head-only presence with my body left behind.

Later, in ketamine sessions, I would literally feel a floating sensation of leaving reality entirely. One moment I'd be in a difficult, blurry place—and then suddenly, I'd be looking up at a starlit sky, weightless and detached. At first, I thought it was part of the medicine. It was. But it was also me. My protector parts knew how to leave. They'd been doing it long before ketamine arrived.

As I kept working, a kind of internal map of where my presence was from moment to moment began to form:

- **In-body**: sensations, emotion, rooted presence.
- **In-head**: planning, analyzing, managing.
- **Floaty**: unmoored, dreamlike, gone.

And just like that, I was learning to *track* where I lived inside myself. The journey had begun, not only into the past or into trauma, but into my body.

I could function and get through my day—even thrive at times while navigating it in some sort of head-only presence. And when things got overwhelming, I floated outside of reality, completely numbed out of everything. My body was not along for the ride, even when being abused during things like training for an Ironman. Maybe dissociation was how I survived that experience!

"Floating Through Space"
–Sia, David Guetta

The sensation of drifting through life — disconnected, untethered, but still moving.

In one of the pre-therapy proprioceptive writings, I wrote about the MS:

3/8/22

I want to go back to the old normal. What do I mean by normal? The way things were before MS. When I didn't notice my body as much. When I thought I was

healthy. But now, I notice my body all of the time
because of abnormal sensation. It is either "heal it"
and get back to normal or ignore it. But I can't ignore
it—not really. What if I befriended it? The MS creates
anxiety, and then I avoid it. If I love my body, it has to
include the MS.

Before I was aware of dissociation as a clinical symptom, I
knew what it was—and I knew I was doing it.

In my first ketamine session, I felt dissociation in real time
—leaving the fear of a dark and scary place behind and floating
up into the stars. I didn't truly realize that is what I was feeling
until later, but I was dissociating even from medicine sessions.

Ketamine is, by nature, a dissociative agent, so it wasn't
surprising that I'd float away from anything scary. It is also
dose-dependent, meaning the experience is heavily influenced
by dose. Really high doses are far more dissociative and psychedelic in nature, while lower doses are more psycholytic. The
effects are enough to soften back the manager parts to work
with what's underneath, but not so much that I can't have some
control over where my consciousness is.

Eventually, I found the right dosage that allowed me to
stay more present in the experience. Once that happened, the
distinction between being in my body (and thus able to work
with body-based parts) and being in my head became easily
tracked. I could also track parts that took it one step further
into what I call the "floaty" place, completely detached from
reality.

Obviously, I don't literally disappear. I just become untethered—from sensation, from presence, from myself. Like a

helium balloon drifting up while my body stays seated in the chair.

Over time, I could trace various states of my consciousness from body to head to floating and back. And the more I worked with the medicine, the better I got at staying in the body.

Now I can track my thinking parts when they start trying to distract me with a flood of thought. The Comedian is especially masterful at deflection, always ready with a punchline when things get too real.

I also can sense when the floaty part is pulling me out entirely. Most of the time I can negotiate a re-entry into the body. Sometimes I can't—often when the work has been intense and I genuinely need a break. The parts are intelligent in that regard.

When in that floaty place, completely checked out from reality, I am not really in my head or my body. I'm still talking and interacting with Ashley, but I don't feel, or think, anything. It is literally like I am in a detached dream state. I am present when the thinking parts are online, but only in the head. There is a disconnection from the body, which, up until the MS, had been largely offline.

The ketamine sessions really help me feel this disconnection between my head and my body.

YouTube — All Ketamine Sessions Playlist

VIDEO CLIP 1
https://bit.ly/KT-Ketamine-Session-Clip1

But even before that, simple parts meditations raised my awareness. This excerpt is from an email to Ashley, prior to my first ketamine session:

> Aug 19, 2022
>
> From a meditation: This time the image was of my whole body with a huge slab separating my head from the rest of my body with a pressure buildup—a block of everything below my neck.
>
> . . . .
>
> There is a big disconnect between my body and my head—the body being shut down in a protective/ defensive position thwarting attack from inside and out. It seems like a dual role for the head/thinking part. One is to keep things going when the rest of me is shut down. But also to keep me shut down because it's protecting me too. The Inner Critic is coming from the head; the body responds to the attacks and shuts down. The head then takes over to keep things going —and a cycle is born.

Now I can tell the difference between head energy and body energy, not only during ketamine sessions but in normal consciousness as well. My center of gravity is different. The fulcrum when I am in the body is lower down in my chest. When I am in my head, it's upstairs.

Not to say that I don't still frequently dissociate, and often it's a while before I notice it. But I have a reference point for when I dissociate, and *when* I am paying attention, I can tell where my presence is.

Sometimes, when things feel too hard and I need a break, I allow myself to dissociate intentionally. Ashley says it's okay to dissociate and numb out when I need to. It is the intentionality of it that makes it different from my unconscious checkouts. I liked that idea.

In an email I sent to Ashley after only a couple of ketamine sessions, I wrote:

> Sept. 14, 2022
>
> What I will say is FUUUUCCCCKKKK. This feels like it's really going to suck. Hurt. I don't want to feel sad—I want to be happy and content. What you said about it being ok to dissociate with awareness—I'm going to use that. Especially right now. I have no one to really go to with this in between sessions. It feels like too much.

I have joked with Ashley that with all my trauma, it is a miracle I didn't end up going down a very different path of addiction or self-harm. But in reality, it's no joke. It's a miracle. I owe that to my thinking parts that chose to escape pain by the pursuit of intelligence and success rather than having to numb out with drugs and/or alcohol. I numbed out with food instead, which allowed me to still thrive.

Eventually, I stopped fighting these thinker parts. After all, they weren't the problem, they were protectors. And like all protectors, they just wanted to be heard. So I wrote to them.

To My Head Managers

> Hi guys:
> Self here. I want to commend you for how well you have managed the system while I have been away. From very early on, there has been a tremendous

amount of pain in my body. From being suffocated as an infant to physical abuse and beyond, every layer added more and more physical discomfort, not to mention emotional turmoil.

The way you quickly adapted and managed to pull all of our energy out of the body and into the head was astonishing and, at the time, was absolutely necessary. You spared me an unimaginable amount of pain. Later, even though the immediate danger had passed, you still sensed the lingering discomfort in the body and kept the energy with you for safekeeping.

In addition, I am just amazed at how smart you became. I owe my career as a physician to you. And even though the Guardian kept things moving with her curiosity, you ran with it. You studied. You analyzed. You calculated every angle.

I also want to speak directly to the Manager who recognizes when it's time to float. Because sometimes it's even too painful to even think about. Now though, as I work with the other Head Managers and the body, I want to let you know that it isn't necessary anymore. Rather, I want you to focus your time and attention on dreaming. I want to dream big. You can, however, dream without leaving. Stay here with the rest of us.

You are without a doubt some of the smartest Managers around. I know I am biased because you are mine, but I have heard many other people say it too. You are freakishly brilliant. I feel so blessed you are my thinkers. Without you, I wouldn't be here.

Kim

FROM FLOATING TO FLESH: ENTER THE BODY

"Movement"
—Hozier

The beauty of embodiment, of how presence and motion awaken forgotten truths.

If dissociation is the flight from the body, embodiment is the slow, uncertain journey back.

I heard the term *embodiment* years ago. *"Being in the body"* sounded like something I should strive for. So I did. I started yoga. I tried breathing exercises. I told people I was doing "somatic work."

At times, I even believed I was there. When someone asked me how I felt, I could answer with something logical about my chest or stomach. It was progress. At least I wasn't saying, "I don't know."

But what I eventually discovered, especially through IFS and psychedelic work, is that I was still only *thinking* about being in my body. The center of gravity in my system, my energetic home base, was still squarely in my head.

Early on, I would get glimpses here and there of what it felt like to actually be in the body, but most of the time those glimpses felt uncomfortable. I used to scoff at people who talked about "feeling safe in the body." I was watching TV on the couch—what could be unsafe? But trauma doesn't check your surroundings. It lives in your nervous system.

After some early somatic work, parts work, and a few ketamine sessions, however, I got it. It turns out my nervous system DID feel unsafe. Because it was living in the past, where it *was* unsafe. I am aware of that now.

It's been only recently that the Exiles associated with the nervous system dysregulation have surfaced with stories. But before that, I was getting glimpses of my Exiles without having a name for them. The somatic clues were there. Even before I met Ashley and started ketamine, my exiles were speaking through the body. In one of my proprioceptive writings I wrote:

March 2022

I feel like a prisoner in my body. What do I mean by prisoner? My body does not feel free. The stiffness in my legs is like concrete. It feels like there is a layer of concrete around my legs. They feel very heavy and unmovable. They are very rigid.

Much later, during my more recent Psychedelic Somatic Interactional Therapy (PSIP) sessions, I would revisit that feeling in my legs, often describing a heavy weight pushing down on them—like they were paralyzed. Different language, same exile.

The ketamine sessions, at lower doses, were helpful at times for connecting with parts but also for being aware of my body. Even after my first ketamine session, I could feel a general sense of contraction and expansion that became a common feeling over the course of several years. I described it this way:

*One thing that comes up is this idea of how I feel in
my body. There is a sense of pressure buildup, of
being contained/trapped in a small space and
pushing out against rigid walls. It's odd, but
sometimes it feels like I am trapped within and need
to release pressure, but at other times it feels more
like a constriction from the outside pushing in.
Sometimes both—but definitely a limited feeling.*

By December of 2022, just a few ketamine sessions into the journey, I was also starting to experience some nausea.

These are examples of some of the early and new awareness of sensation in the body. I was inhabiting my body for brief periods, and I was learning quickly that it didn't feel good in there.

Once I really started listening, I discovered that my body had a whole lot to say.

In an email to Ashley after a ketamine session that December, I wrote:

Trust my body.

It was such a simple statement but was a huge shift. My prior relationship with my body was to either ignore it at best or, at worst, abuse it. Now, I was shifting that relationship. I was listening and starting to trust what it was telling me. The lump in the throat, the constriction in my chest, and the nausea in my gut were all clues that would eventually lead me to my Exiles.

With each medicine session, and the work in Ashley's office in between, I grew more aware of my body and its language.

The more awareness, the better the tracking. This means I was beginning to associate parts with body sensations, and ultimately, with the stories behind them. The stories are fragmented and I don't have conscious memories, but I don't need conscious memory to believe that something bad happened. The body says it did, and as Ashley has told me on more than one occasion, the body doesn't lie, or as Bessel Van Der Kolk says in his book of the same title, *The Body Keeps the Score.*

In more recent medicine sessions, I've been able to inhabit my body more. The imprinted trauma in my nervous system has been evident despite a lack of conscious memory. And trust me, it is not comfortable, but I am learning to stay with it rather than dissociate. And by staying with it, I'm ultimately working to shift it to a more relaxed and safe state. The hope is that, over time, I will get to where it does feel safe to be in the body most of the time.

With each medicine session now, when I go into the body, I feel it. And I stick with it as long as I can. Then, I feel myself leave the body for a bit and take a break. I can now go back and forth. Sometimes it is intentional, sometimes more involuntary.

The important thing is that I am getting very good at tracking my parts and where my presence is during the medicine sessions. With that increased awareness, the medicine sessions are becoming even more effective.

I now completely understand what embodiment is, how it feels, and why it's important. When my body and my head feel safe and work together, it is magic. I wouldn't be able to write this book without my body on board.

CHAPTER FIVE

Meet My Exiles—
Hello from the Prison of Pain

"Hello"
—Evanescence

Loneliness and grief personified —
the mind as its only companion.

A PORTAL OPENS

I was making slow and steady progress with my parts while also getting more and more nuanced messaging in my ketamine sessions. I thought I had answered the question about what lurked beneath the surface: emotional neglect resulting in cPTSD.

But then everything changed during a ketamine session in November of 2024, when I suddenly and unexpectedly slipped into the energy of a protector/Manager part. As the dose was wearing off, I got very panicked and anxious. Without much conscious control, I started pleading and crying, repeating phrases like "please stop looking," "please don't go in there," and "please stop." It was clear that there was a highly agitated protector in my system who was deathly afraid of me discovering something that I was getting dangerously close to.

I came out of it and moved on with my day but remained disturbed by the experience. What had just happened? I had another ketamine session shortly after, and I set a gentle intention of exploring it. What happened next was just as disturbing, if not more so.

This time, I didn't just meet an Exile; I became it. I felt a similar panicked energy fueled by confusion and fear. Again, without much conscious control, I started saying "stop," "stop doing that," and "please stop" like a child would.

"What just happened?" This was clearly something more than emotional neglect, and it caught me completely off guard. Those sessions seemed to open a portal into more intense and direct communication with my exile parts that up until then had seemed distant.

PSIP: Enter the Chest Exile

It was at this point that we introduced PSIP. Although I didn't have any explicit memory of physical or sexual abuse, it was becoming clear that I was dealing with more than just emotional neglect in my system. The body was reliving fragments of prior experiences, sometimes quite intensely. Looking back, I see the early somatic sensations as a foreshadowing of a deeper story. Now, for the first time, I was coming face to face with the Exiles underneath.

In a way, PSIP is a physiological counterpart to experiencing an exile and reliving their trauma. The method involves identifying the little things we do that trigger dissociation away from growing discomfort and inhibiting them. Those micro-escapes could be a deep breath or sigh, clearing the throat, or other small body movements. For me, taking a deep breath is a frequent micro-escape. That act of inhibition takes the nervous system back into the moment of the trauma—into the pure sympathetic fight-or-flight response.

That pure fight-or-flight state is too energetically expensive to stay there. So eventually, the nervous system has to go elsewhere—and there are two possible paths. The first one, the one I have taken my entire life, is to dissociate. The other, the preferred one, is to return to a normal "safe" resting state. The goal of PSIP is to teach the nervous system the path to safety from within the trauma. This is accomplished through interaction with a safe and present other who wasn't there when the trauma happened.

When I first started doing PSIP, inhibition of the deep breath resulted in an overwhelming squeeze in my chest and throat. It would get so intense, I simply couldn't take in any air.

Saying "I can't breathe" through a closed throat and tight chest became a common experience in session. I would also get the very real sense that I was in the energy of an infant. My vocalizations during the session would even sound like a baby. At some point during the third PSIP session, it came into focus. The Exile shared some context.

I got the live, animated image of a pillow coming down over my face. It was an intense moment of terror, but, as I commented during the session, it all finally made sense. This Exile had been nearly suffocated as an infant.

I started to put it together. Without going into too much about specific details, the context was enough for me to fully understand my infant-age Exile. In the following PSIP session, I almost immediately went into this exile and literally relived a moment of being suffocated, to the point of going limp as if I had died. The Exile had shown me what happened, and then it showed me how it felt in my nervous system as a baby. The felt experience of the Exile and activation of the nervous system in the PSIP model are the same phenomenon.

In IFS, a traumatized Exile is stuck in the past at the moment of injury. It still thinks you are the age at which the trauma occurred, and it still believes the danger exists.

In PSIP, the theory is that the nervous system is stuck in the trauma, looping between moments of activation and dissociation. The end goal of the work I am doing with this Part is to unburden it and at the same time teach my nervous system safety.

Meeting this chest exile and gaining insight around physical abuse I never knew I had suffered was shocking. However, it was clear to me that this was not the Exile I had met in the previous ketamine sessions. That panic I experienced before was coming from some other part I had yet to meet. A few ketamine sessions later, however, I did.

Meeting the Gut Exile

This other exile didn't live in my chest; it lived in my belly, and it let me know it was present with a physical symptom just as distressing as the chest squeezing. I started having waves of nausea when this gut exile would surface. I also began having sensations in my pelvis, and my body would involuntarily move into a defensive position with my hands over my crotch. This Exile felt a bit older in energy than the baby who had been suffocated.

I knew something was definitely wrong, but I didn't have a sense of what had happened. Even at the time of this writing, I don't know specific details or have explicit episodic memories. I am working with embodied, somatic memory and clinical patterns consistent with trauma.

I have, however, put together enough somatic pieces to understand that this Exile likely suffered some sort of sexual abuse. Another exile. Another shock. Another discovery of something below the surface that I had zero conscious awareness of.

Now I had two distinct exiles surfacing in medicine sessions with different wounds and different energy around them. I would go back and forth between them in a single session. I would know when I'd shift from one to the other. As I started experiencing the Exiles in such an embodied way, my Manager parts became more distinct in their efforts to distract me. It was only after I experienced the pain that I could notice pulling away from it. And it is a Manager part that takes over when I dissociate.

Enter the Comedian

As the nurse walks toward me with the next ketamine injection in hand, I start singing, "Come on baby, make it hurt so good," joking about the sting of the needle. I start laughing at my humor, and before I know it, I am laughing hysterically. Laughter being infectious, Ashley and the nurse both join in. I stop long enough to tell them, "I should be charging you for the entertainment."

One Manager part that makes a frequent appearance when things get uncomfortable is the Comedian. I find myself in the Comedian's energy often, laughing or telling jokes when things get uncomfortable. Imagine a group of therapists all gathered at a therapy convention sitting around discussing with each other who has the worst, most "fucked up" client. Ashley says, "Let me tell you about Kim," and when she finishes, all the other therapists agree in unison, "You win!"

This is a joke I told during one ketamine session as I was struggling with how dark and twisted things felt. I was genuinely feeling broken. But what came out was a joke and a bunch of uncontrollable laughter.

YouTube — All Ketamine Sessions Playlist

VIDEO CLIP 2
https://bit.ly/KT-Ketamine-Session-Clip2

One time during a ketamine session, Ashley asked me what would happen if I inhibited my breath again. I said, laughing, "Well, we know what will happen." Like it does in my everyday life, the Comedian is clearly working hard to protect me from wherever I am going in that intense moment. Humor is a brilliant protector. I am a genuinely funny person, but I also use humor to mask a lot of uncomfortable situations.

VIDEO CLIP 3
https://bit.ly/KT-Ketamine-Session-Clip3

While the exile energies were becoming more distinct during medicine sessions, they became more blended while working with them outside sessions. As I navigated through my day, I could sense their shared fears, pain, and deep isolation. On a deep nervous system level, the traumas and Exiles were clearly distinct, but on an emotional level, it was the impact of the trauma that came through. And the impact of both—dissociation, anxiety, using food for comfort—was remarkable similar.

So I speak to both exiles in the same way and often get the same responses. I picture both exiles being confined in what I call a "prison of pain," immobilized in invisible walls that were never meant to exist. Born of separate traumas but united in the same longing—to be seen, understood, and healed.

The Letters: Befriending and Building Trust

What follows are brief excerpts from a series of letters I wrote to both exiles as trust began to grow.

This first letter emerged after a ketamine/PSIP session where I felt my envisioned exiles go from a smaller version of me deep down to full size as if it merged with my outer layer of skin. Ashley thought it might represent a transition from the baby energy of the traumatized exile to adult form. That is probably partially true, but as depicted in this letter, it was about the part leaving its cage and expanding to feel what life can be like now. That moment, however, was fleeting.

Letter to my Exile 1

> *I have this part of me, tucked away inside a glass box —tiny in stature, but the box is even smaller. I see you contorted and contracted to fit within a space that was always too small to hold you. I feel you unable to move, like a magician strapped into a straight jacket. And the other day, with my attention, I was able to dissolve that glass surrounding you—yet for a while you did not move.*
>
> *Why? You were free! There is fear always. It has just shifted from always being trapped, tucked away safely from harm but fearful of what can't be, to the fear of facing and feeling the outside world with the risky unknown. After all, it was the risky unknown that put you in the box in the first place. Or maybe you just didn't even know that the box was gone.*

Perhaps both.

But in a few moments of your absolute courage and trust to meet me, I felt you stretch your legs and arms, slowly and gently expanding into the frame you were always meant to exist in and grow with. For once, your boundaries and mine were one and the same. And for once, we felt real. It was a fleeting moment of wholeness that reminds you—no, US—that wholeness has always been available and can return. We remember it even if it doesn't seem like we do.

Our body remembers what it is like to have all of us occupy it fully and unified rather than contracted inward in fragments to avoid the risk of feeling the outside world. My boundaries meet that world but do not feel it because you have always been the sensitive one, the feeling one. The truth is I need you. I always have, but I forgot.

You protected me by sacrificing yourself to save me from pain, yet I abandoned you.

All those strong feelings were never meant to be trapped. As you expand into me and your feelings meet the world around us, I promise to be here with you for every step and feel every emotion right alongside you. I can protect you. Maybe not from ever being hurt again. In fact, you will almost certainly be hurt again.

But I can promise I will protect you from ever being alone with it again. You never have to return to that box trapped with the hurt. I am here now and forevermore.

You can face the fear, knowing you aren't alone. And if it helps, know that I have fear too. It's natural. But now, we can expand together. Facing the fear of change, hand in hand.

Between medicine sessions, I started to experience physical symptoms of my exiles. I had known for quite some time that I would stop breathing, and that wasn't new. Now waves of nausea were waking me in the middle of the night. This next letter was born out of paying attention to the nausea during those random moments. It was also recognizing how in the past I had largely ignored it and even actively shoved it back down.

Letter to my Exile, Part 2

> . . . I have been thinking about you. I am now starting to understand your language—speaking through nausea. I understand now how when your waves of pressure rise up from your cage, trying to escape, I shove you down with a swallow. I also now understand some of the point of eating. I can also feel the hurt in the pelvis, legs, and feet. I know that for a long time I have ignored them to make the pain go away. And that has worked beautifully for so long, but I never realized that by ignoring them, I was ignoring you—a big part of myself. It further deepened that wound of abandonment you feel. I am so sorry I left you alone in it. But I am starting to pay more attention, and I am feeling you in them now. You don't have to hold things in anymore. Use the nausea, use the waves in the legs—use whatever you must/can to tell me your story. I am here, I am listening, and now I can understand better what you are trying to say.

This next letter was written after a particularly hard ketamine session where the body's implicit memory of some sort of sexual abuse started taking form. I struggled to understand, and I lacked any context of an actual story. There was a tender balance of wanting to know what happened but understanding the timing of if/when my exile ever shares it.

Letter to my Exile, Part 3

Hi. It's me again. Hopefully by now, you recognize me when I knock. It feels like you do, and that you are trusting enough to invite me into your world for brief periods. I am so thankful for that.

I understand how awful it has felt to be stuck there in that place, and I feel awful that you have been there all alone. I know you are slowly trying to tell me more of your story, little by little, and I am doing my best to accept it, believe it, honor it, and help you transmute it.

In time things will come into view enough that you will feel like you have gotten through to me in a way that unburdens you from all the pain. That love and joy I talked about is right around the corner. Stick with it. Stick with me and keep inviting me in. Each time you do that and let me come in just a bit further, I understand just a bit more.

We will get there, and it will be worth it, I promise.

The last letters were written after moments of feeling the exiles physically outside of ketamine sessions—after middle-of-the-night wake-ups. And for the first time, the Exiles were talking not just somatically, but I could also hear their voices, reflected in the fact that these are more conversational than my earlier letters.

A Night with my Exile:

To my dear Exile:
I am here. Tonight, I want to step into your world. I sense you almost all of the time, and I know you are hurting so badly. The only thing I can do right now is just be with you and let you talk. Yell, scream, cry, or just sit in silence. It is all ok. There doesn't need to be any fear at all. I come with nothing but love and presence. I am going to feel what you want me to feel, hear what you want me to hear, and speak only when you want me to.

Hi Kim:
It has been so long since I first cried out to be heard, to be rescued. So long that eventually I just gave up and couldn't cry out anymore. I have felt like help would never come. I just accepted that pain would be my life forevermore. It has been there so long that I can't imagine life without it. I try to tell myself this is real—I still have a hard time believing it. Are you really here? Self? Are you really here to rescue me? I need to know. Because I cannot survive another disappointment. That is why I have been slow to open up to you. I don't fully trust yet. The promises you make, things such as joy, love, and peace—I do not understand them. My entire existence has been nothing but unimaginable pain.

You have gotten my hopes up before. Times when it seemed I might be heard or seen, only to realize it was only partially and very temporary. That makes it hurt even more. And it's why I have been so reluctant this time around to trust you. But I just NEED someone to hear me. I NEED someone to see me. I

*NEED someone to love me. And I am giving it one
more try.*

Morning with my Exile

*Good morning, my beloved. I felt you last night. The
searing physical pain from the loneliness rising from
deep in the pelvis. You showed me just a glimpse of
how much it hurts on a physical level. It felt like my
body was shredding in half for just a brief second. At
first I wasn't sure if I was awake or dreaming, so you
sent a bit more to make sure I knew it was real. And
did it help reassure you to know that I felt it and
knew it was you? That I am listening?*

This collection of letters traces the arc of evolution
through my understanding of my exile parts. It began with early
glimpses—moments of awareness and disorientation as I first
encountered them in ketamine sessions. I learned about their
traumas, felt their somatic distress, and noticed how invisible
and isolated they had been. The isolation was revealed in an
indirect way by the protectors who rushed in to try to shield
me from them.

Over time, I began to understand and work with their
unique language: the nausea, the breath-holding, and the
subtle anxiety their pain spoke through my body. Eventually, I
stopped trying to "fix" them and instead started to sit with
them in their pain, not only in medicine sessions but between
them as well.

Writing these letters helped me embody that shift from
being unaware to hearing them to feeling them—and finally to
being with them. The ultimate goal of this work is to rescue

these Exiles, bringing them out of their past, frozen in trauma, and into the present, full of connection and love. IFS calls it unburdening. That rescue is still unfolding. But it is only made possible through the act of communion and presence that developed through these letters. There will be more. It takes time, and the trust is only just beginning.

With language and relationship forming, the work turned toward unburdening. And I am confident that it is only a matter of time before my Exiles feel safe and loved enough to leave their prison of pain for good—and join me in the life I have promised them.

These Exiles are shrouded in terror. Later, I would meet an Exile shrouded in shame . . .

CHAPTER SIX

Touch and Connection

BUILDING CONNECTION AND SAFE TOUCH

"Grow as We Go"
—*Ben Platt*

An affirmation that growth can happen within a relationship, not apart from it.

I've never been a hugger—and am not crazy about being touched in general. Like I said earlier, I have no vivid memories of a warm hug from my mom or of holding my dad's hand. Not having it felt so normal to me that I didn't even realize I was missing it.

Through my work with Ashley, I began to realize that it was, in fact, abnormal to be so deprived of touch all these years. I wrote to her a few days after my first ketamine session, where she first introduced touch.

August 28, 2022

I don't remember much hand-holding, hugging, or touching when I was young. We didn't do any of that— or say, "I love you." It was implied. I see just how little human touch I have had over the years. I'm talking about casual/friendly touch, but sex is also cold and for the most part unenjoyable for me. It's hard for me to stay present in it.

I also soon realized how the simplest touch caused me anxiety. I didn't have a massage until the age of thirty-three, and I didn't schedule it because I wanted a relaxing experience; I scheduled it more out of desperation due to daily tension headaches. It was the start of what would eventually be a life-long practice of routine massage.

The first several sessions I wouldn't let the masseuse touch anything other than my neck, shoulders, and upper back. It took four sessions before I would allow a full body massage, and even then, it took many more sessions before I could actually relax.

At the time, I saw that this wasn't exactly normal, but I attributed my modesty to body image. I didn't have a clue that touch was actually activating my nervous system below the surface. Looking back now, I see how even then, my trauma patterns were in full view.

Ashley was patient, always asking first and letting me feel into things at my own pace. As I progressed in therapy, so did my capacity for allowing touch. Most commonly, she put a hand on my shoulder, or if I was lying down, on the back of my neck (which was surprisingly soothing).

It was slow going. It took almost two years, but I was eventually able to tolerate her sitting close to me on the couch, the sides of our bodies touching. Most of the time, I wouldn't think to ask for touch. Early on, if she asked if I would like to be touched, I'd quickly say, "No, that's okay." But eventually things progressed to where Ashley would ask me if I would like some touch, and I'd agree.

As I started to get more comfortable with touch, I began to ask for it unprompted, but I would always wait until there were only a few minutes left in my session to do so. That allowed for a quick escape.

As my comfort level grew, I found myself really wanting it. I would think about it while driving to her office—craving the sensation. However, I always stopped myself from asking for what I really needed/wanted. My Manager parts, always on alert to protect me from vulnerability, would speak up and stop me from asking. I eventually started messaging her ahead of the session to name what I needed so I couldn't back out. That approach really worked, and now my sessions are full of touch work.

My last session, in fact, started with a big hug followed by an entire hour of her sitting right up against me on the couch—then ending with a hug. I started out afraid and anxious about touch, and then it became tolerable. Now, it actually feels warm and inviting. To say that I have come a long way would be the understatement of the decade.

Touch has been helpful for me, but it's never required. Consent and collaboration matter more than any technique. Ashley was always mindful of getting consent, and I learned to listen to my body for a yes or no.

In many ways, my struggle with touch mirrored my struggle with relationships. I don't mean romantic ones, although those were pretty low in quality as well, but relationships with friends and family.

I had always been one to avoid conflict at all costs, putting my needs and feelings aside to avoid having a difficult conversation. I'd never learned to have emotional conversations. I instead kept to myself with everything except the superficial details of life.

Until therapy, I didn't realize just how abnormal that was. Talking to someone about my feelings felt like stepping into a horror movie—my instinct was always to run.

I also think back to my first encounter with therapy, around the same time I had my first massage (circa 2004). It was during a spiral into a deep depression, and a friend insisted I go. At first I refused but relented when she practically dragged me into a therapist's office. It was three or four sessions before I said *anything* to this therapist, let alone talked about any emotional debris. Ultimately, I developed a good working relationship with Melissa, and therapy helped me get out of the depression. But it didn't reach the things that lurked below. What it *did* do, though, was get me into endurance sports, and the rest is history.

My latest trip through therapy, however, has been different—not only with psychedelics and somatic work, but because there has been an emphasis on relationship. Working with Ashley has increased my ability to stay in one now—through emotional moments and difficult ones. I've learned that my well-practiced avoidance tactics don't just keep me from conflict. They also deprive me of the positive aspects of a relationship: care, nurturing, warmth, and touch.

Ashley began weaving in aspects of relationship, within proper boundaries, to help me learn the good parts of being in one—but also how to repair it when things go sideways, or in therapy language, when there is a rupture.

"I want you to tell me when you get mad at me," she said early on in our work. "It's the people who don't tell me they're mad at me who end up quitting."

A big part of expanding my relational capacity *is* repairing the relationship when things go awry, and I remember that when my wounded parts get triggered by something Ashley has done (redirecting me with a gentle boundary, not responding to an email, etc.).

I have always chosen to stay, despite a few times when my Manager parts have told her to fuck off—in my mind anyway. My protector parts try to throw walls back up after a minor rupture and threaten to quit therapy. But I remember what she told me—and I am not a quitter. So I gently tell my parts that I am not quitting and that Ashley cares for me, and I walk back into her office.

I've even gotten comfortable enough with my relationship with her that I tell her about these times when they happen. I have learned that Ashley always stays, and that is something my system has never really experienced before.

As I continued to sit in Ashley's office week after week, my relationship with her shifted several times. Initially, I saw her as an authority figure who was going to sift through my deepest, darkest secrets and help me sort them out, which made me feel somewhat intimidated. It was hard to be vulnerable, and in a lot of ways I felt childlike when I was in her office.

My protective Managers worked on the outside to make it challenging to dig deep early on, and the wounded parts on the inside were carrying the torch of shame. It was that shame energy of my childlike parts that predominated how I felt in her office. Even though I physically towered over her, I felt very small.

Eventually, other Manager parts became fixated on healing from a more clinical perspective and took over. I was fascinated by the process and by the techniques and theories behind my healing journey. I was still reading books and listening to podcasts, trying to diagnose and treat myself. When I began to feel more of that Manager energy in her office, she became more of an expert consultant rather than my therapist.

My comfort level continued to grow, but it wasn't until the touch therapy really took off that I started seeing Ashley more in the role intended all along: a caring, nurturing, and present figure acting as a placeholder for my Self energy and for a real relationship outside of her office.

As I became more attached to Ashley as this type of presence rather than just my therapist, I could feel the shift and shared my thoughts with her in an email. Here is an excerpt:

> And what has come up is this subtle shift in how I FEEL about therapy/you. For a long time it was "I trust you," but I kept myself kind of level in terms of allowing you to help me. But the framework in my brain was entirely within myself… Then this last session there was a shift in how your presence was felt—not just a warm spot on my shoulder but a person. Since that time, there has been this subtle but growing shift into seeing you as more than a warm hand and more than an "impersonal" therapist, but as a comforting figure…
>
> There is also that part that fears becoming too attached, dependent… I have never had anyone that I just allowed to take care of me—emotionally… It is like I am reverting to a kid just wanting someone to take care of me after a bad dream.

Therapy was working. While change was gradual, my system knew early on that I was in the right place and that Ashley could hold that system in a caring and nurturing way. I wrote to her after my very first session:

> One of the things I sensed was the little girl feels a little
> safer to feel some pain in the container you are
> providing than with any other talk therapist—safer than
> even with just me.

Physician and author Gabor Maté developed an entire therapeutic method called "Compassionate Inquiry," wherein he believes healing can only occur in an environment of safety and compassion. In Ashley, I had finally met someone who held the compassion needed for my system to begin to heal.

Connection in Action

While things were shifting in how I showed up in relationship in Ashley's office, they were also shifting at home.

One of the first things Ashley did before I ever met with her in her office was send me a Spotify list of podcasts that discussed psychedelic therapy and IFS. On one, a guest described his experience with neglect. I hadn't had the awareness around my own emotional neglect yet, but what struck me was how much I resonated with his story—especially when he started talking about his pet and how he was more attached to it than his parents. I *really* resonated with that.

My dog, Lexi, was the one living being I ever truly connected with. Later I would make the connection that my parents were more emotionally attached to the family dogs than to me. I recently found a picture from when I was about six years old. I was sitting on my mom's lap on one leg, and the family dog was sitting on her other leg. She was leaning toward the dog with one arm wrapped around it. The other arm was pinned to her chest—not around me.

That one picture speaks volumes about my mother's attachment, or lack thereof, to me. After listening to that podcast, I had a sense that I was heading in the right direction.

LEXI: LOVE RECEIVED

"All I Want"
—Kodaline

A mourning of love and the aching absence of someone dear.

Lexi was a Yorkipoo I got as a puppy. She was a consistent and steady presence for me whenever times felt challenging. Her role was to love me, and I leaned on her. Yes, I loved her dearly, but she was the stable one, and I was the needy one. She was with me through the most tumultuous times of my life: job changes, my parents' house fire, breakups, and endurance events, including Ironman. And she was with me through most of the last three years of therapy. Many nights, the only thing that got me through was a look and a kiss from my Lexi.

Not long before the writing of this book, she started to show a rapid decline in her cognition. Mostly deaf and partly blind, she was confused a lot. After many sleepless nights, I made the heartbreaking decision to assist her transition. I arranged for a vet to do an in-home visit, and I asked my good friend Jo to be with me during the moment Lexi was put to sleep and also to stay the night with me afterward. She agreed.

The arrangements were made, and the nights leading up to it were gut-wrenching. I stayed up and lay on the couch with her, crying. I was allowing emotion to pour out like never before. I didn't cry nearly as hard when my mother passed.

Eventually, the day came. Jo sat next to me with her arm around me, and I held Lexi while she took her last breath. It was the most heartbreaking moment of my life. I cried uncontrollably for quite a long time, not worrying about what it looked or sounded like.

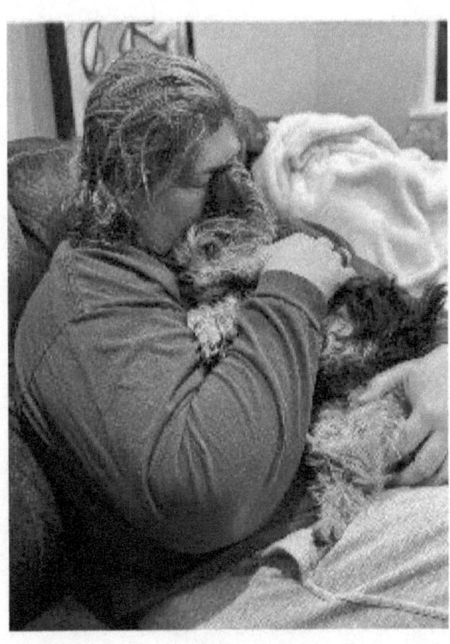

Jo consoled me and eventually gave me a long hug. After I calmed down, I lay on one side of my L-shaped couch, and Jo sat on the other. We put a movie on. I asked her to stay up with me for a bit, and while I lay there, she put her hand on my shoulder and rubbed it in a loving way while I talked.

Sounds like a pretty natural way for a friend to show up in a tough moment, right? Well, this was the first time I'd ever asked for help, received it, and felt comforted by a friend in a highly emotional moment. While I was mired in extreme grief over the loss of my beloved dog, I couldn't help but also have a sense of awe at how far I had come. I was allowing someone in. I was allowing touch. I was expressing emotion. I was asking for what I needed. I was sitting in my grief rather than trying to numb it out.

Underneath it all, I finally *felt* heartbreak. I could feel the ache in my chest, which was something I didn't feel when either of my parents died. Lexi was such a blessing during her life, and she gave me one last gift in her passing: the ability to truly grieve.

DOBBY: LOVE GIVEN

"Grow as We Go"
—Ben Platt

*Dobby and I are learning and growing
as we go — together.*

Shortly after Lexi passed, I asked her to send me my next dog. I knew I would get another one, but I wasn't sure what or when. A friend of mine works with an animal rescue group and tried to convince me that I should adopt a rescue. I scoffed, not wanting a dog I hadn't raised myself. I had heard nightmare stories about rescues with behavior problems, and I didn't have the energy for that.

Not long after, as I was driving, I got a message from Lexi: "I was here for you. You need to be there for your next dog." It hit. I *had* to adopt a rescue.

I looked online at various rescue dogs locally and visited with a few. The friend who brought up adoption in the first place wanted me to meet a dog she thought would be a good fit for me. I wasn't convinced but agreed to meet him.

Feb. 2025

I open the door, and standing there is Linda, a foster parent for animals with the Wichita Animal Action League (WAAL). Next to her, less than a foot off the ground, is a shivering, short-haired brown chihuahua mix. His big brown eyes are wide open, almost bulging, as he cowers slightly behind Linda. I invite them in. "Meet Zac," she says.

They walk to the couch, Zac sticking close to Linda, tail down between his hind legs the entire way. She sits, reaches down, and takes off his leash. He jumps up on her lap. Still shaking, he is reluctant to leave it.

I call his name. Zaaacccc. I pat my leg, calling him. He doesn't move. Finally, I get up, walk into the kitchen, and get a bag of treats off the counter. Now I have his attention. He jumps down and slowly walks toward me. I reach down with a treat and call his name again. He inches toward me, then dives in to grab the treat from my hand with his mouth, immediately darting away before he eats it. I try it again. Same thing. He finishes chewing and then jumps back into Linda's lap. After a short visit with Linda, she stands up to go. Zac exits the way he entered. On a leash, tail tucked between the legs and almost hiding behind Linda.

Not once did Zac get close enough for me to even pet him. He was clearly anxious and fearful of the experience and of me. But there was something behind the big brown eyes that sparked something in me. "Please love me," they said. Linda had mentioned that he'd been in foster care for over a year. That's a long time for a foster animal. That night, I thought more on it and decided to meet him again.

A few days later, Linda brought Zac over for our second visit. It started the same way the first one did. But then, he slowly ventured off Linda's lap and across the couch to mine. He did it reluctantly, but he did it. He stayed for only a few seconds, but long enough for me to pet him. That was enough.

Those eyes had spoken, and now it was clear. He needed love, and I was the one who was going to give it. Zac was my dog.

I adopted him and over the next few months worked on building trust with him—trust that I wouldn't hurt him or leave him. And ultimately, I worked at simply loving him. Lexi had been there to love me, and now I was giving love to another dog in a way I wasn't capable of before.

One day I came home from a particularly hard ketamine session and sat on the couch, soothing Zac. I thought about how things had come full circle: I was working with Zac as Ashley was working with me.

I was not, however, fond of the name "Zac" and wanted to change it. His big eyes, floppy ears, and meek demeanor reminded me of Dobby, the house elf in the Harry Potter movies.

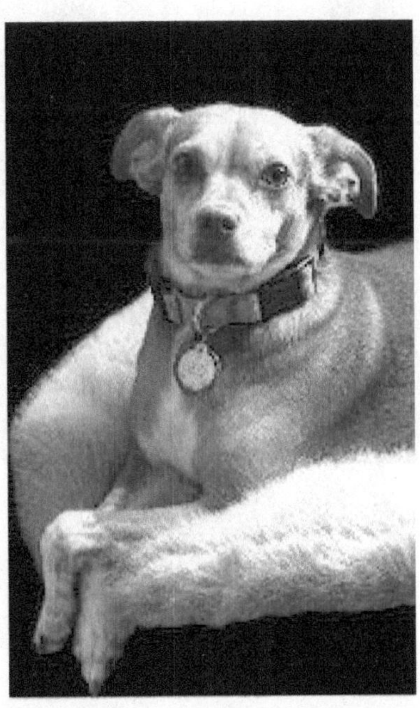

So I changed his name. He is now my Dobby and I love him dearly. He has adjusted to his new home and his new name and is now a frequent visitor to my lap. He leaps with relief and excitement at my return home and does what I call the Dobby Dash when I walk through the door.

I look at him sometimes and smile that he got a mom who understands trauma and a dysregulated nervous system better than most. A mom who can now actually give him something he desperately needed: a steadfast and loving presence. Lexi will always be planted firmly in my heart. She taught me how to be loved—and how to grieve. Dobby is teaching me how to stay—and how to love.

From Connection to Rupture and the Tender Exile Underneath

"You Say"
—Lauren Daigle

A battle between lies of worthlessness and the fragile truth of being loved.

As I expanded my capacity for touch and real relationship with Ashley, the traumas were surfacing in the medicine sessions. This work was unsettling and disruptive to my system that had grown cozy and comfortable. I found myself *wanting* support and comfort from Ashley, and I was asking for more of her between sessions with points of contact through emails. And while she never inferred that they were too much, the parts of me that feel like they are too much and a burden started talking louder.

I was opening up to Ashley more both in session and in

emails, and some parts were feeling alarmed at my new vulnerability. I was also feeling confused about boundaries. How much was too much?

A perfect storm was brewing—and it blew into a hurricane when, at the same time, Ashley was the most unavailable she had ever been, due to growing obligations in her life and practice. If that wasn't enough, the storm hit a category five when I had to leave home for an extended period to start a new job. I was extremely stressed by the demands the job was requiring, and I was going to be away for a couple of weeks from all the support I had built.

Shortly before leaving for the job, I had a couple of unsettled nights, during which I wrote long emails to Ashley. I never expect a reply unless I specifically ask for one, and I didn't specifically ask. But this time was different. I needed a reply and didn't realize it. And the reply didn't come.

Within a few days of leaving home, while in the throes of this incredibly challenging job transition, my insecure parts grew louder. Thoughts like "I am a burden," "She probably rolls her eyes when she sees another email from me," and "I am too much" flooded my brain and spiraled into shame. And while a response from Ashley might have calmed them, it wasn't going to come, at least not right away.

And—it would have only been a temporary brace against the storm.

THE SATELLITE CALL

"Satellite Call"
—Sarah Bareilles

*A message of love transmitted into the dark,
reaching someone who feels alone.*

The energy behind this shame spiral felt a bit different than it ever had before. I sent out a call: Self asked for all parts to speak up. After working through the layers, I met another Exile, one who felt softer and more tender than the others. Up until then, all the parts I'd met had been through some sort of physical abuse.

The emotional neglect component I started with in the beginning had become overshadowed and forgotten. This new Exile I met held the neglect *and* shame I was feeling. The letters that follow are my conversation with the insecure parts as well as a letter to the Exile part I met, who I call my Tender One.

It took intense medicine/PSIP sessions to meet my Exiles who were abused physically and sexually. But all it took was getting quiet with my insecure parts to meet my Exile who had been neglected all along. In retrospect, I believe it's my Tender One speaking in that first letter; I just didn't know it at the time. Her voice had always been there, just muted beneath the harsher, louder ones. It was her burden of shame that had been behind a lot of the insecurity in relationships I had suffered throughout the years.

Conversations with my Triggered Parts

Hi, Self here again. I have been sensing some anxiety in some of you recently. I know I am under a lot of stress at the moment, more so than in the recent past. I know I am asking a lot of you right now in family therapy. I know everyone is tired and unsure of things. We have been here before and have always gotten through the only way we know how: survival. I already know you are all masters at helping me survive. But this time, I am asking you to help me do it differently. I am asking you to lean in and tell me what you are feeling and needing so that I can tend to you in ways that offer something different than survival. I am asking you to not only let me in, but I have also brought some others in to help me help you. That is a lot that I am asking, and up until now I am so thankful that you have been working with me to find a new way through life's challenges. But now I sense some resistance, and I want to open the floor to your concerns.

Hi Kim:
I am a Firefighter, a part you know really well, but we haven't officially met. I am the one who protects you from getting let down, from disappointment, from abandonment—essentially from getting hurt again. And I see what is happening here. You have really been opening yourself up to the other people you have invited in and exposing all of us to a lot of danger. It was ok for awhile and up to now I have been fairly quiet and allowed you to slowly move into it. But now, things have shifted some and the depth

to which you are allowing people in is getting concerning. Danger warnings are too much to ignore now and I have to step in. So I am pleading with you to back off. Stop sharing. Stop going to these outsiders. The risk of hurt is growing to great to ignore.

Hi Kim:
Managers here. We are also a bit alarmed at the exposure. We have shared a lot with you and with your friends. But our willingness to share only goes so far when the things you have promised us, like support and comfort, seem scarce. We warned you not to be a burden to Ashley. It just feels like we are again, and now we are going to push the support away just when you were starting to convince us it was ok to ask for it.

Hi guys:
Thanks for sharing your concerns so openly. I get that I have not received a response to my request for extra support this week, and I understand it is causing you all some distress. But rest assured, it is there. I feel it. I get that you are unable to. Honestly, I wouldn't expect you to yet. Like a baby just learning to walk, the process is clumsy, and they frequently fall.

This is something entirely new that you are having to learn, and I can understand that current circumstances would cause you to stumble. I will admit, they are extreme. The support I asked for is truly there. I haven't heard back, likely because of timing, logistics, and honestly, because the person supporting me is very wise and knows exactly when and how to respond to give me the support I need. It is ok. Really.

Trust me that I know what I am doing, that the outside support knows what they are doing, and that you are all held tightly even though right now it might not seem like it. I am going to keep going. I am going to keep being vulnerable and open. I am going to keep asking for help and support when I need it. I am going to rest in the knowledge that it is always there even when it isn't. And most of all, I am going to keep moving toward all of you with love and compassion. Of that, let there be no doubt. So everyone take a deep breath and relax. Everything is going to be ok.

The Whisper

After sitting with the last letter for a bit and leaning into the shame, I could finally sense this tender exile buried deep inside. I could hear:

"I'm in Here"
—Sia

The raw voice of a part trapped in pain, begging to be seen and rescued.

I responded to that whisper.

Letter to my Tender One

Hello, my little Tender One:

You aren't like the others. The other exiles have hardened, and while they too are scared and lonely, they have a cold bitterness to them that comes from years of being confined in a prison of pain. And they have sturdy and loyal protectors that are surrounding them and walling them off from the system. They have learned not to need anyone or anything to survive in their primitive and painful existence. It is easier for them that way.

But you are different. You have such a tender presence. So angelic and childlike. You have not become bitter or angry, yet you have the deepest and most raw wound of them all. All you ever wanted was just to be loved. You have only existed in the shadows of neglect. With each moment when love was needed and not found, you felt more and more unlovable. I can see your hurt and confusion. Shame took advantage of your vulnerability and tenderness and tricked you into believing you were not only unlovable but also completely invisible. How could you not believe it? No one ever gave you a reason not to.

Over time, I see how shame slowly grew into an all-consuming fire within and around you, suffocating you of what little oxygen you had. Eventually, you became completely invisible to the system, surrounded by so much shame that it seemed you were one and the same. None of the other parts saw you. I couldn't see you. While the other exiles were screaming, you were crying—and yet no one heard you. All we could see and hear was the shame, which grew so strong it spread like a wildfire throughout the system.

Shame has but one goal: to keep you hidden away, invisible and silent. I have been working hard to loosen shame's grip, and as I have done so, the fire is diminishing, and I can see you now. I see your wounds. I hear your cries. And most importantly, I feel you need for tender love. You don't ask for much. I can hear you now saying, "just please love me."

I have been trying to reach you for a while. Every time I get close, I too find myself enveloped by the smoke of shame and end up pulling back. But the shame is lifting and the smoke is clearing. I don't know if you can hear or see me yet. I hope you can. I see you cowering at being discovered. You are so torn between desperately wanting love and being completely ashamed of needing it.

I know lately you have felt a bit more exposed and visible. I feel you reaching for me at times and reaching for others. I also hear the cries of shame louder than ever before. You feel you are too much— yet at the same time fear you are never enough. You are afraid to be seen. You feel like a burden to all those you touch. Most of all, seeking the comfort and nurturing you so crave, and frankly deserve, puffs shame up, and the dark cloud starts swirling around you once more.

I want to say that you were never unlovable. You are precious and worthy of more love than you can even imagine. It was the people who were supposed to love you that let you down. Myself included. You did nothing wrong. You weren't bad. Your existence was something to cherish and celebrate, not invalidate into silence and shame. And you were never invisible, just cloaked in a cloud of smoke that obscured your cries.

Most of all, you are not too much. You are not a burden. You belong and deserve more love than you can imagine. I am here now, and while I cannot make up for the love you never got before, I can and will make sure you are loved now. You do not need to do anything or change who you are. You belong here, and you are loved simply because you are worthy of it.

After writing these letters, I could feel my energy shift. I had let go of the anxiety around feeling too much. Not to say that the shame and the "I'm too much" energy won't return in full force in the future, maybe even tomorrow. This wound is old and deep, and my Exile is timid. But I have now met the Exile underneath and can return to her. By spending more and more time with her, perhaps there will come a day when my exile has shed the burden of shame and *I'm too much* or *I'm not enough* becomes simply, *I'm just right.*

Love, Intimacy, and Desire— The Deepest Layer of Shame

THE UNLOVABLE

"Iris"
—*Goo Goo Dolls*

*The ache of wanting to be truly seen,
even if misunderstood.*

This is the chapter I almost didn't write. Because there's something profoundly sad about spending a lifetime thinking you are unlovable to your core.

Sure, people liked me. I was funny, outgoing, and often the life of the party. Even when I was young. Well, right up through yesterday. The self-fulfilling prophecy is this: when you think you are unlovable, and your parts act accordingly, you *are* unlovable. Because the very parts that can give and receive love are tucked away so deep that no one can crack it, not even yourself.

That was me. Tough exterior. I used to joke (thanks, Comedian) that I have already met my soulmate, and I told him to fuck off. It's probably true. I may have missed out on the love of a lifetime because I couldn't let him in when he came knocking at my door. I also have a tough interior. I use the present-tense "have" because of all my trauma patterns, this is the one still most alive.

Before therapy and before my Ironman, I recognized that I was walled off from love and romance. I had dated off and on through the years, but nothing that lasted more than a few months.

I found guys I felt superior to in intellect or status so that I didn't feel so small in the relationship. I also always found guys who were as emotionally blank as I was, so there was never a risk of having to truly be seen. It was a subconscious pattern that in retrospect is quite clear.

I set an intention of improving in this area of my life. I wanted to open myself up more. I wanted to allow more love. I wanted to finally have a relationship with a man in which I could be emotionally open and more present during physical intimacy.

MARK: THE ONE, UNTIL HE WASN'T

"And So It Goes"
—Billy Joel

The quiet risk of offering your heart, knowing it may break.

Mark was an RN I met through an online dating app. I am not one to spend a lot of time chatting online; I prefer to see if there is interest and meet in person. The way I saw it, time was precious, and fifteen minutes at a coffee shop sitting across from someone was far better than two weeks of online texting. So, after a brief conversation online, we agreed to meet.

I got there early and anticipated when he would walk

through the door. When he did, my heart skipped a bit. His profile pictures were cute, but he was even more attractive in person. He was strong. Manly. The first impression was yeah, this is going to be different.

As he approached me, I stood up and we briefly hugged in a way that new acquaintances might. We then walked over and ordered coffee. The conversation was light, and I took him in. He smelled freshly showered and clean. Bald head. Just the right height. Muscular and a great smile. We sat down and, both being in the medical field, had no shortage of things in common to discuss. I don't even remember the conversation much because I was drawn to him.

We went on a second date. And a third. By then we were making out in the the car in the Outback Steakhouse parking lot. And then we were kind of dating, although we never really made it "official." We were physically compatible, and I found myself enjoying sex a bit more than I ever had. I remember one time after we finished, I lay there in his arms, and we talked about dreams for the future. What? That was a first. I really thought I was progressing. And I was, just not as much as I thought.

Turns out even though I was seeing things slightly differently, I still managed to find a man void of emotional depth. We avoided some of the real conversations, even something as simple as relationship status.

I met Mark shortly before starting my Ironman training. And as time progressed and my training got more physically demanding, I had less energy and desire for sex. In fact, it fell off quite a bit.

About six months after we started dating, Mark took a trip

to Arkansas to help his mom, who was showing signs of cognitive decline. He needed to assess the situation and said he'd be gone for a couple of weeks while he sorted things out. We met for coffee the morning he left, after which we hugged goodbye in the parking lot. At the time, I thought it was "Goodbye and see you soon."

What happened next was surreal. He never came back.

He got to Arkansas and decided to stay. He left me hanging for several weeks, telling me he was delaying his return, then getting more and more distant until he finally admitted he wasn't coming home. Home was Arkansas now. It was a gut punch that only landed like a glancing blow thanks to being in the throes of Ironman training. Ouch, I thought. Oh well, what is my workout today?

By November, when I queued up at the starting line of Ironman Arizona, Mark was a faded memory. A failed experiment that meant nothing. I never really processed what had happened. I didn't have to because I still had survival mechanisms in place that were excellent at burying things.

Recently, during a psilocybin journey, Mark surfaced, and I retold that story to the guide. This time, however, I experienced deep and guttural grief. "He just never came back!" I cried. It was clear that was an unprocessed wound: the "he left because I am unlovable" wound.

Revisiting the New Lens

About a year after starting my ketamine journey, I took a short writing course with Jeff Brown, a lawyer turned writer and one of my favorite authors. I was hooked on his work after reading his memoir, *Soul Shaping.* If a lawyer could pursue his passion in life, so could I.

One of the exercises in that course was to write about a romantic encounter. I paused. I didn't really have one to write about. Yes, I had dated, but nothing special. Certainly not any kind of match-up passionate enough to write about. So I varied mine a bit.

Spring 2023

> The prompt is to write about a romantic encounter. My version of this is a bit different. I am 50 years old. One would think that in all that time I would have at least one passionate romantic encounter to describe. But I don't.
>
> Instead, what I have are long-held internalized feelings of shame and worthlessness that, over time during my younger years, built significant walls around my heart. Walls that I didn't even know existed for the longest time. I always just thought I was just unlovable. Weight issues and, in general, having the self-narrative of being fat and unattractive contributed to a life without love.
>
> I have dated in my later years, but it is usually short-lived and lifeless. I find men who are also emotionally unavailable, and that allows me to be superficial, never having to reveal what lies beneath the surface. It is an interesting yet painful place to be, to have an achy longing for love and connection yet feel so afraid of it and disconnected from it.
>
> There have been countless nights of lonely tears. My thoughts wander to how the world around me is moving, yet I am standing still, just out of reach of

connection to something that might make me feel a part of it.

Touch is an interesting thing. For so long, even just a hug with a friend was uncomfortable and avoided. Holding children intimidated me. And sexual encounters certainly created high anxiety. So while I have had them, I can see how I check out during them. Not really feeling anything. I have never, in all my 50 years, kissed or been kissed by anyone with any passion or feeling behind it. I have never felt comforted by just a simple thing such as a hug.

Through the work I have done, I have been able to progress from avoiding touch to allowing it, but it still is very neutral in that there is no sense of connection or comfort from that touch. I have genuinely never felt loved. Never. And for the longest time, the cliché "others can't love you until you love yourself" just dug the dagger in deeper, as self-love also felt like a theoretical concept just out of my reach. It is a lonely place to be indeed when life is void of love and of connection.

As humans, we are hardwired for that, until those wires are grossly misconnected when it matters most. As I awaken to my inner processes that have created such a demon, I understand why. My parents were both very emotionally unavailable and riddled with shame themselves. From very early on in my life, before conscious memory, I have been internalizing shame. Layer after layer.

As a teenager, when social events and dating became front and center to life, the shame compounded into a demon that has completely dictated my life, even up to now. So many buried feelings of sadness and loneliness. So much confusion. So much negative self-talk. All of it internalized in a one-person conversation with myself. I never had intimate emotional conversations with anyone, not even my parents, about anything I was thinking or feeling.

I am the dictionary-perfect version of "survive by dissociation." Survive I did. One could argue (at least I will anyway) that I actually thrived despite it. A successful doctor. Thriving in the eyes of a world I do not even feel a part of. In my inner world, I am a giant collection of miserable cells. Cells so miserable, they now remind me of their misery each and every day with multiple sclerosis and the sensations and limitations that illness brings.

Understanding why I am this way and overcoming the deep anguish of loneliness are two different things. In fact, I would say that the sadness has intensified as I start to grieve all these years where my soul longed for but lacked connection. All of the years where my soul has fantasized about even just a hug on a difficult day, yet nothing. Not even compassion from myself until recently. As I grieve, the compassion for myself is growing. It springs forth out of understanding and grief. How does one overcome such feelings of isolation and loneliness? It feels like this grief may never end. I am working on it, but it's deep. The roots are strong. And therapy can only go so far. I long for a meaningful connection with another soul that allows me to even feel what connection can be.

Can I, at 50, saddled with weight and chronic illness, hope to find love? Even IF I do heal to where I can allow it? Or is the best I can hope for to connect more with myself to quiet the intensity of loneliness?

Can I slay this beast or simply tame it?

I am healing. But it is slow. And in the darkness of the night, I know there is a dawn, but it requires a tremendous amount of hope. Hope for a better future. Hope for connection. Hope for love. Hope for passion. Hope for wholeness. How much hope can I muster? Some days it feels faint. Others, it springs eternal. How long can one spend life just hoping for something better, or even just tolerable, before hope fades?

It takes a mighty strength to hold on to hope through the tears and the anguish. My soul aches and grieves for what might have been but is so resilient, and even through it all, is still sending me enough of that hope to keep going just when I need it most.

My parts were exceptional at protecting me in this area. My Firefighter part made sure I consumed enough calories to keep my body undesirable. My Guardian part made sure I rested in the comforting thought that I didn't need anyone. And when things got uncomfortable, my Comedian always made sure I had a joke or two at the ready. My unlovable Exile was guarded with every single ounce of energy my system had. And in the moments of absolute despair in the loneliness, the suicide Firefighter was on call, a call my guardian wouldn't allow me to make.

In that writing, I named the ache I had felt for so long. A longing was growing. But even in that writing, I recognized that I wasn't quite ready to allow love. I wrote it after the relationship with Mark but before the realization of how it impacted me. I also wrote it after I had started touch therapy but before I had gotten to the point of being comforted by it. Long before that comforting hug Jo gave me after Lexi died. I still had a long way to go.

SHOW ME

"Show Me"
—Idina Menzel

*A song about daring to reveal the hidden self
and trusting someone to accept it.*

In the years since I wrote that letter, I have learned how to love myself more. I have learned to allow and receive care and comfort from others like Ashley and Jo. But I know my next step is allowing in love in a more intimate way. I don't mean just sex, but to have someone who says "I see you" and "You matter to me." Someone who is there at the end of the day and not just when the schedule allows. Someone who doesn't have you in the middle of the pack on their priority list.

My relationship with Ashley is in a very specific container, and even within that, she has other clients. While Jo loves me, she has a husband, children, siblings, and parents who all need her attention too. I come after them. That is as it should be. But I want a connection where I am first. Someone who can say I matter the most. I have never really experienced that, not even with my mom. For as far back as I can remember, my brother was always more important. Not that she didn't love me, but I was the strong and independent one. I didn't need her as much as my brother did.

Allowing someone in at that level still feels like choppy water. But I feel like I am finally ready and able to navigate the rough sea. I am indeed lovable. But the sticky thing about this is the realization that body image still plays a role. Before, it was "I am unlovable." Period. Therapy has helped, and now I see how lovable I am. I see the wounds and shame for what they are.

But the things that make me lovable are on the inside. My personality. My traits. My very soul. I am interesting. I am caring and kind. I am funny. I am loyal. I am freakishly smart. I am all of these things. I might be the dream catch for a guy, because I am drama-free and I love sports.

But there is something that still hinders me. Shame around how I look still gets in the way. Because *that* is still unlovable. Overweight. Chronic illness with MS. Who would want that? No one would stay long enough to see the lovable parts underneath.

Body image is something I thought I dealt with before Mark. With him, I was more open and freer with my body. But I was still emotionally shut off and could separate from the shame. AND, my body was fit. I was training for an Ironman, after all.

Now I am in touch with my parts and can feel that part of me is still alive. The Inner Critic is having a field day with the weight I've gained and tells me the MS is a deal breaker. Will I find love? Stay tuned because I sincerely hope I do, and that book will be juicy. And yes, I can finally say that I *deserve it.* Not just someone who stays—but someone who stays with passion.

LOVING MYSELF WHILE WAITING FOR PASSION

"Passionate Kisses"
—Mary Chapin Carpenter

*A joyful insistence that passion
and pleasure are birthrights.*

For now, while I patiently wait for that passionate kiss, I am just going to rest in loving myself better and loving those body-shamed parts until they can let go. Only then can I truly let myself be seen. Fully.

As I have become more embodied and opened one layer at a time, sexuality is an area that still feels full of shame. But I have learned to allow myself to feel pleasure in an embodied way. The emotional depth is there. The relational capacity is there. The ability to feel pleasure (embodiment) is there. The final frontier is to allow myself to be fully seen. To believe that someone will see me, all of me, and love me just as I am.

I will close this chapter with another letter to my tender Exile, the part that holds all the shame. The one who longs for connection and love but also needs to stay invisible to feel safe:

Letter to my unlovable Exile—my Tender One:

Hello, beautiful One:
For so long you have felt unlovable. You were

unlovable because your wounds were hidden. It is hard to love what you can't see. And the lack of love only strengthened your resolve. It only hardened your outer shell. Now though, I have dug through all the layers, and I can see you. I can feel you. I feel your longing for connection. Your ache: a canyon of grief for love. I also see the shame you have held for feeling so unlovable. Admitting you want love is dangerous.

But I want to let you in on a massive truth. You are loved. You do not have to feel like you deserve it —there is no element of worth to this. You are loved simply because.

But you are shy—and hindered by a deeply held belief that love is conditional on how you look. And while I agree that what makes you so stunningly beautiful is all of the love and qualities you hold on the inside—you are also beautiful on the outside. The more light that shines through, the brighter you get, and the light is all people see. I promise you. The world needs your beautiful light to shine, and when it does, people will notice. And they will say "you are beautiful" from the moment they see you.

There will be people who don't leave. They will stay and see all of the layers. And someday, someone special will see it all. For now, I see you. And that is enough. Feel my love and spread from there.

With so much love,

Kim

CHAPTER NINE

Pleasure Belongs Here

"Soak Up the Sun"
—Sheryl Crow

An invitation to embrace life's simplest joys with gratitude.

This chapter began with an orgasm—and a revelation.

Did that get your attention?

Yes, I said orgasm. And no, this isn't just about sex. But it starts there, because that's where shame tried to hide the loudest.

I was alone, and in an exercise of embodiment. I was feeling into my body with presence rather than performance. Something opened.

A quiet surrender.

A flood of longing.

The real kind, not the woe-is-me, I'm alone kind.

The aching, honest, please-see-me kind.

And with it came tears: deep, ancient tears.

Grief, shame, and an almost unbearable vulnerability I had never let surface before.

And I swear to God, as I lay there tearful and soft, my Comedian part whispered: "Oops . . . I did it again." Sorry Britney.

Pleasure used to feel dangerous and shameful. And humor used to mask it. Now it feels . . . honest.

That was the moment I knew: this chapter had to be written. My initial manuscript did not include this chapter. I had danced around the edges but managed to avoid going into the deepest, darkest layers of shame.

But true healing asks us to include *everything*.

Even the parts we've been taught to silence.

It is time to bring the unspeakable out of the shadows. And it feels liberating. This is stuff I haven't even broached with Ashley yet. Alchemy in real time.

And so, while not the focus of this book, I want to say this plainly:

Women's pleasure is not shameful.

Women's longing is not too much.

And women's bodies are not simply vessels for pain—they are portals for truth.

Sometimes, the most profound insights don't emerge from agony but from the gentle courage of allowing ourselves to feel.

This chapter was born in that courage.

The knowing that I had to write this wasn't just intellectual; it was embodied.

And the *release of shame afterward was palpable*. Not imagined. Not aspirational. *Real.*

While sexual pleasure is important, and still taboo for so

many women (myself included), this chapter is also about something bigger:

Pleasure in its broader, sacred form.

The warmth of sunlight on your face.

A mug of tea between your palms.

A hot bath. A deep laugh. A dog sighing beside you.

These are the kinds of pleasures we're taught to dismiss.

At best, we're too busy surviving to notice them.

At worst, we've been taught to feel *guilty* for enjoying them at all.

But as Bessel van der Kolk writes in *The Body Keeps the Score* (Chapter 18):

Pleasure and engagement are antidotes to trauma. They help bring the body back into the present.

And Adrienne Maree Brown says it even more plainly in *Pleasure Activism*:

Pleasure is the point. Feeling good is not frivolous. It is freedom.

Pleasure isn't a luxury.

It's medicine.

And it's mine.

I'm still learning to remember that every day.

But I've found my own daily practices—tiny portals back to myself.

And yes, the aforementioned orgasm is up there. And today, it opened up a portal into the body that released a ton of shame.

But most days?

It's just lying in the grass. My dog at my side. The sun on my face.

That, I think, is the greatest pleasure of all.

I am making time for it and no longer apologizing for it. *Any of it.*

PART III

The Resistance and Doubt

CHAPTER TEN

This Is Bullshit!—
My Hardworking Skeptic

"Doubt"
—Twenty One Pilots

*A cry of uncertainty, haunted by disbelief,
but still pleading not to be forgotten.*

This wouldn't be a complete cross section of my internal world without a nod to my Skeptic who has become particularly prominent as I receive more information from my Exiles. In every ketamine/PSIP session in which trauma and the Exiles surface, there is also a prominent "I don't believe it" response from my Skeptic.

YouTube — All Ketamine Sessions Playlist

VIDEO CLIP 4
https://bit.ly/KT-Ketamine-Session-Clip4

VIDEO CLIP 5
https://bit.ly/KT-Ketamine-Session-Clip5

In one memorable moment, I was experiencing strong energy in my pelvis. It was hard to deny what was happening. During that intense moment, I actually became my Skeptic and yelled, "That's not enough!"

VIDEO CLIP 6
https://bit.ly/KT-Ketamine-Session-Clip6

It's hard to convince this part that any of what is coming up in the medicine sessions is real. Outside those sessions, the Skeptic also gets quite loud in the moments where there is touch: either Ashley simply sitting beside me in physical closeness or with her arm on my shoulder. Every time she provides therapeutic touch or talks directly to a childlike part, I hear the Skeptic's voice saying, "This is bullshit" or "This is stupid." It tells me that it's stupid for a fifty-two-year-old to be sitting there engaging in such childish things.

But the fact of the matter is, in those moments, it is my childlike parts that are getting to experience something they never got when I was younger. And I also know that my fifty-two-year-old needs nurturing. So, I listen, but I don't act on the things the Skeptic is telling me. I let Ashley sit next to me. I even ask her to.

This letter is to my Skeptic, with whom there has been a softening of its harsh bullshit meter in recent sessions. While it still makes itself known, it is becoming more accepting of both the Exiles' story and their needs.

Conversation with my Skeptic

Dear Kim:
I have been with you for a long time, and over the years I love that you have always listened to me. I work very hard to protect you from embarrassment, from getting your hopes up, or setting yourself up for disappointment. In general, I keep you protected from harm by always bringing to your attention flaws in any situation that could expose you. We have had a good working relationship up until recently—I warn, and you pull back. That's how this works.

Now though, you have been going around and talking to other parts, and they are telling you some ridiculous stories. And worse yet, I sense you wanting to believe them. These stories can do nothing but cause you pain, and I wish you would just listen to me when I say they are made up. It is so much easier for you that way. I don't know what I have to say to convince you they aren't real. Something has changed.

I also see you inviting in connection, even allowing and sometimes asking for touch, and now I have to work overtime to protect you from that. Touch used to be dangerous, and now, well, it just leaves you vulnerable. I want you to see just how silly and embarrassing it is to sit on that couch with Ashley and have her put her arm on your shoulder. Things are getting serious, and I have to speak up. I know you can hear me when I tell you that "this is bullshit" and "this is stupid." It is the only way I know how to get through to you. But you ARE NOT listening to me!

I am pleading with you. Heed my warning. Go

back to that world of cynicism and disbelief. It is easier to stay numb that way, and numb is good. It may not feel awesome, but at least it doesn't hurt.

Hi Skeptic:
I hear you. And I appreciate your desire to protect me. I really do. But you have kept me stuck in hopelessness for some time because the biggest lie you convinced me to agree with was that things will never change. Now, as I sense things ARE in fact changing, I have to take a step back and reassess other things you tell me.

You are right; I HAVE been talking to other parts and listening to their stories, and I cannot deny the evidence. What they are telling me is compelling and heartbreaking, and I cannot turn away from that in some effort to avoid the pain. You admit that you deep down actually do believe their stories—and your attempt to invalidate those stories as false is actually the falsehood.

I don't blame you. I understand why you do it, but that doesn't mean I have to keep listening to you. Times are changing. As for your loud voice during sessions with Ashley around touch, I do hear you. And while I am tempted to listen and shy away, the parts that have been denied for so long are just louder. And I have to listen to them. I don't want you to go away. On the contrary, I need you. There will be plenty of times ahead where I do need a bit of a warning shot that maybe I should pause and think about something before jumping in. I want your bullshit meter to stay plugged in, but I need you to recalibrate it. I need you to do that. The Exiles need you to do that. And honestly, you need you to do that.

You are working way too hard. The next time you want to call bullshit, I invite you to take a step back and just witness for a moment. I think you will find that the pain you fear, while real, is manageable. Even transmutable. I can handle it, and helping your sibling parts is worth the risk. I love you.

VIDEO CLIP 7
https://bit.ly/KT-Ketamine-Session-Clip7

CHAPTER ELEVEN

Change—
The Gas and the Brake

"I CAN'T CHANGE."

"December"
—Sarah Bareilles

*A meditation on letting go of an old self
and stepping into change.*

I've repeated that phrase more times than I can count. Every promising attempt flames out. Every cycle, no matter how inspired it begins, eventually brings me right back to where I began.

When I wrote in my journal, "I am mad at me for who I am," that core conflict became crystal clear. I would have periods where it *seemed* like things had changed, but I would ultimately always end up where I started. Or at least, that is what I always told myself. Exhibits A and B: Look no further than my grand spirals after my parents' house fire and again after my Ironman. In both cases, I fell back into the old eating patterns, weight gain, and depression.

I've repeated this pattern numerous times throughout my life. Each time I end up back where I started. Each cycle adding another notch in the belt of "I can't change" with a big "I told you so."

Early on in my journey, I pondered the question, "Why can't I change?" I didn't get very far.

My initial insight was simply because this is who I am. Whether it was genetics, upbringing, a lifetime of examples, or all of the above, it was firmly ingrained in me that the qualities I was trying to change couldn't be manipulated. They were in the very core of who I was, a place I lacked access to.

"I want to change, and to do so I need to change my core belief pattern, but I don't know my core beliefs" is a paradox I couldn't escape from. I set out on a search to learn why I had such a strong belief that I couldn't change.

It turns out, there are some pretty interesting reasons.

As I began to frame change through the lens of IFS, I leaned into what parts played a role in this belief. Just a few weeks after starting therapy with Ashley, I wrote to her about a parts meditation I did focusing in on "I can't change":

Aug. 19, 2022

The guided meditation asked to focus on a prominent thought. I chose "I can't change." He** asked me to find it in the body. It was clearly in and around my head. My head was spinning a bit. Then he asked to find an image for the thought. It came pretty quickly. It was just a random scribble with hard/heavy strokes.

There was more to that meditation, but from this excerpt, it is clear that I was meeting parts resistant to change from very early on.

**He is Richard Schwartz, narrating guided meditations from his audiobook, *Greater Than the Sum of Our Parts*.

I eventually discovered an interplay between my Historian and my Skeptic. The Historian keeps meticulous records, not just of my life, but of everything that came before me: my genetics, my family history, etc. The Skeptic wants proof that I *can* change, so he turns to the Historian.

And all the Historian can offer is the past. The historian has plenty of evidence to pull from and the Skeptic doesn't ask many questions. It takes the Historian at face value, never asking what might be missing from the records or what's changed since the last entry. It's a vicious cycle: "See, I can't change; I told you so, because look what happened before."

BUT WHO WOULD I BE?

"Happy"
—NF

A confession of fearing happiness because it feels unfamiliar and unsafe.

I learned that parts at my core feared change because they were clinging to an identity built around my trauma. This deeply rooted identity was based in shame, worthlessness, being fat, being unlovable, etc.

Ultimately, underneath the lack of ability to change was a fear that without the identity I'd held for so long, I would simply cease to exist. Somehow my system knew that all of the temporary identities I had built over the years were just that—temporary, and not a threat. The old standby never failed them, and they didn't want to let go of the safety net.

In addition to the scared identity parts and the collaboration I mentioned between my Historian and my Skeptic, I have a Guardian part who is hell-bent on creating change. This part has an altruistic intention to bring about change for the better but is forceful, persistent, and frustrated when there's no desired outcome.

I also have an Inner Critic who would blast me for my inability to do the things necessary to bring about change. When I want to lose weight, it says, "Put down the cupcake and go exercise—you know better, and you don't do it because you're lazy and lack self-discipline." The hopelessness in me says putting down that cupcake won't matter, because I won't ever lose weight anyway. Hopelessness leads to lack of action, which leads to lack of change. It is all a cycle that, until the patterns are broken down, just feels like one rigid belief: "I can't change."

HOPE AND CHANGE

"Hope"
—*Shinedown*

*A reminder that hope is a lifeline,
not a weakness.*

Without hope, there can be no change. Early in my first psilocybin journey, as I was just starting to feel the effects of the plant, my system was fighting it. I was anxious. My protector parts were having a hard time backing off enough for the plant to gain access. The longer the resistance went on, the more my Historian and Skeptic stepped in. I said out loud to the guide, "This isn't working. This isn't going to work. I can't change." At that point, the guide asked me to lean into that phrase, "I can't change."

As I did, I had a stark realization. I still remember the sinking feeling in my chest when it hit. "Oh, there's despair at the end of that road," I said to the guide. When you are angry at yourself for who you are, and you stand firm in the thought "I can't change," it leads straight into a pit of hopelessness from which there is no return. Eventually, I sank into the medicine and had a decent first descent into psilocybin. But the most profound moment of the eight-hour day was hitting that despair. It was a life-changing awareness.

I came back from that psilocybin journey refocused on the idea of change, now framed through hope and despair. I was also working on intergenerational patterns at the time, and I realized that hopelessness was a deeply ingrained one that I had seen play out in my mother's and my grandmother's lives. And I was slowly watching it take over mine. When you are hopeless, there is no reason to try. And without trying, there will be no change.

I thought back to a conversation I had with my Pilates instructor, Aliesa, prior to my entering therapy with Ashley. Aliesa didn't just train me in pilates; she was also a friend and a therapeutic ear. She heard all about my struggle—with myself, my parents, and life. I spent quite a bit of time talking about my mom and how she never did anything to help herself.

One day, while going through an exercise on foot and ankle mobility, I commented that the exercises were pointless because my rather rigid ankles would never get better. "It's hopeless," I said. Aliesa looked at me and in an unassuming manner simply said, "I imagine that's how your mom feels."

Mic drop. It hit like a brick to the gut at the time, but I forgot about it as soon as I left the studio. Now, though, it's a profound memory. There was another pattern underneath my lack of ability to effect meaningful change: hopelessness. And it felt like I was the one to break that generational curse.

Not too long after my psilocybin experience, I had an MDMA journey with the focus being on my intergenerational dynamics. I had a vision of being a Roman warrior in a helmet with the red feathery stripe down the middle. I was leading my family and my ancestors into battle. Not with swords and arrows, but with determination as my armor and my weapon. A determination to live in hope—a battle against that generational despair we had come to know and internalize.

It was one of the most vivid images I have had in a medicine session. Shortly afterward, I had a friend conceptualize a tattoo of that Roman woman warrior with a shield and added the words "Always choose hope." Within two months of that MDMA session, I had a beautiful tattoo on my right arm to remind me.

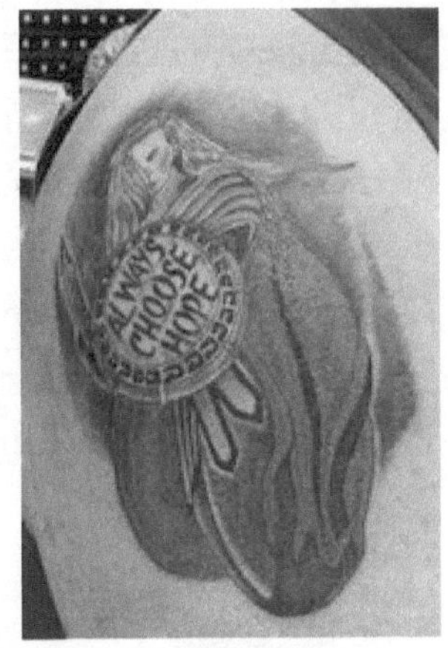

SPINNING THE TIRES

"Courage to Change"
—Sia

*A call to face fear head-on
and choose transformation.*

"I have been trying so hard for a long time," I said as I cried.

During a period of intense emotion, I was lamenting a lack of outward change and the seemingly unattainable easing of struggle in life. What came up during this part of the journey was a nudge to explore why I seemed to always be going nowhere despite a tremendous amount of effort.

Then it came to me in a metaphor. I had been trying to drive the car of change with one foot down, pedal to the metal, on the gas. But with the other foot, I was slamming down hard on the brake. I was saying and doing a lot of the right things to move forward. But underneath, I still had parts working hard to slam the brakes on change. I was simply spinning the tires.

The following is a letter I wrote to my Historian after the most recent psilocybin experience:

Letter to My Historian

Dear Historian:
I have been steadily working with your brothers and sisters to effect change in the system. Yet, I sense a tremendous amount of resistance from you around it.

You have allowed some change—small things, and I do appreciate that. But as we approach some bigger changes like healing the MS, weight loss, new relationships, etc., you have dug your heels in. I want to understand.

Dear Kim:
I have collected a lot of data over the years, dating all the way back to when you were born. I have tracked episodes of abuse as an infant. I have watched shame take up space and grow over the years. I have witnessed and recorded countless instances of disappointment and heartbreak. And I have made notes about all of your prior attempts at change, of which there have been many. In all cases, you end up right back where you started—where you have belonged all along.

I have even done research on your parents and their parents and have noted many patterns that repeat themselves across the generations of your family. Everything has led me to the conclusion that it doesn't matter how much you try—you are stuck in a mold that cannot be broken. You have always been and will always be overweight. You have always been inconsistent with self-care. You use food for comfort, thanks to my firefighter brother, and that will never change no matter how many times you temporarily willpower your way out of it.

Even now, as you tell me things are changing, I see that nothing of consequence really is. You STILL eat for comfort. You have been alone your entire life, and despite many attempts to be in a relationship, you always end up alone. The more you try to change these things and fail, the more I dig in. I only do it to protect you. You risk further pain and disappointment when you allow yourself to believe that things can change. AND even though there is some minimal possibility that change could be achieved and be worthwhile, there is a much safer path of staying the same.

It may not be fun or pleasant, but it is familiar and comfortable—and that is worth everything. Without the pain and misery, who would you be? That is all you have known, and there is real uncertainty in what would happen if you let go of that. Staying comfortable is better than risking any more pain. You may not realize it, but while you have ignored the pain in your Exiles, I have been quietly paying attention, and I see it all. There is no way I can let that pain out. So when you say you want to understand, I have many valid reasons for not wanting change. I am proud of the fact that I have protected you from it all these years.

Dear Historian:
Thank you for explaining. I would simply like to point out that all of the records you have kept up to now have had one thing in common: My Self is missing in them. But I am here now. I am working to transmute the pain in my exiles.

Just start with allowing yourself to imagine brief moments away from the record room to look around and see what is going on elsewhere. I think you will be surprised. Most of all, I want you to feel into my energy and allow yourself to believe that I'm real. I appreciate all that you have done for me to protect me and my other parts, but it is time for you to be able to start recording a different history.

You don't have to rewrite the past.
Just stop pre-filling in the future.
Leave it blank and let me do the rest.

With so much love,
Kim

I can't erase fifty years of history in a single letter. But hopefully over time I can get my Historian to see the small changes that are already occurring and slowly release the brake. The Historian isn't wrong. Things have been hard and patterns have repeated. But this time, change isn't coming from a desperate part or inner critic-driven willpower; it's coming from Self. *Yes, this time IS different.*

The Lighthouse

I have a pretty good idea why up to this point I haven't shown much external change. On the inside, there has been a tremendous amount of change. Despite it, my Historian and my Skeptic only focus on outward things. Same with the Inner Critic. But when Self leads, I'm able to focus on the inner changes that have happened and have faith, patience, and hope that outer changes will follow. Which leads me to hope, because change and hope are somewhat interchangeable. They are both really verbs representing mobilization.

I've discovered that when I spiral and seemingly take a step backward in my healing journey, it's because I've fallen back into the hopelessness pattern that things will never change. It makes the present situation that much more acute.

Living without hope when faced with chronic illness,

chronic loneliness, and a lifetime of painful memories is a horrible place to be. And that's when my suicide Firefighter becomes the loudest. My suicidal part, a Firefighter who steps in during those moments of despair, still shows up—just less often. But just as my suicidal Firefighter surfaces, so does my Guardian part who quietly whispers to the system, "Nope, keep going." I am thankful for my Guardian part. It is like a lighthouse. No matter how deep the waters of despair get, the pilot light of hope just never goes out.

When hope is present, even the most dire situations don't feel so heavy. Hope helps mobilize into action. I don't mean big actions, but just something as simple as taking a deep breath.

Even before my epiphany with the psilocybin, I knew the importance of hope. In an email to Ashley after my second ketamine session, I wrote:

Fall 2022

Hope is a fleeting thing these days. Some
days I have it. Some days I don't. It is amazing
how quickly a ketamine session can boost it.
Tonight, there is hope.

There have been plenty of ups and downs since then. But the important thing is I always come back to hope like the lighthouse in the dark.

And now, I have gone far enough that Self energy can take the pilot light and turn it into a flame that burns stronger and brighter even during the dark days.

THERE'S ALWAYS
ONE MORE TIME

"There's Always One More Time"
—B.B. King cover by Harry Connick, Jr.

*A soulful reassurance that there's always
another chance to try again.*

No matter where you are in your journey, there will be moments when despair is knocking at the door. And if there is one message in this entire book that is worth highlighting or writing on a Post-it note and sticking to your mirror, it is this: keep going. Cling to hope. It is the lifeline to your future, no matter how dire your present situation is.

And if you're in a moment like that now, let this final song hold you the way it held me.

Because as long as that pilot light is still flickering, there is always one more time.

CHAPTER TWELVE

Layers

*The cry of someone whose body carries pain,
longing to be understood.*

I have been overweight as far back as I can remember. Even in my youngest elementary school pictures dating back to kindergarten, I was overweight. I have spent my entire life resisting the weight. Fighting it. Hating it. Shaming myself for it. Embarrassed by my parents for being overweight themselves. Growing up, I internalized my weight as my identity. And I internalized the reason for being overweight as a deep and permanent character flaw. As I got older and started working on myself, I started to realize there were layered patterns that allowed me to increasingly separate myself from the weight.

Like Mother, Like Daughter

The first layer I encountered was learned behavior. I had learned my eating patterns from my parents. I was in medical school before I knew what a vegetable was. Growing up, the only veggies were corn, peas, and potatoes; I was living away from home as a medical student before I tried any others. We ate fast food, pizza, and homemade grease bombs, followed by sweets for dessert. This was normal to me.

I also watched my parents stuff their feelings down with food from as far back as I can remember. I was not consciously aware of it, but my nervous system was keenly tuned to it. While it was more acceptable than being a personal flaw, the disadvantage of poor eating habits from learned behavior still wasn't enough to have any self-compassion for the weight. My critic then argued that once I knew better, I should act better.

It's the Gut, Silly

Then came the day I discovered the connection between the gut microbiome and obesity. For those unfamiliar, the microbiome is a vast ecosystem of bacteria, viruses, and fungi that live primarily in your gut and help regulate everything from digestion to immunity to mood. A disrupted microbiome, especially early in life, can contribute to inflammation, metabolic issues, and even struggles with weight and emotional regulation.

I was set up for an altered microbiome: I had severe colic as a baby, a sign that I already had an altered microbiome (dysbiosis). My pediatrician told my mom to give me Karo syrup to treat the colic. So I was fed high fructose corn syrup in my formula bottle at every feeding. Being formula-fed instead of breastfed can alter the microbiome. Throwing Karo syrup on it is like pouring kerosene on a fire.

Now I had a physiological reason why weight had been my lifelong struggle. I could separate myself a little more from my weight, but I still struggled with internalized shame and self-hatred over my weight. It was the inner critic's most prized topic.

I continued to fight it. I started eating better, began buying organic foods, and limited my calorie intake. I lost weight and was feeling better. I started training for endurance events and ultimately took on the challenge of an Ironman. At the age of forty-seven, I was the most fit and healthy I'd been my entire life. If willpower were the answer, I would still be trim and fit. Attributing weight issues to lack of willpower is one of the most damaging things our society has done to people who suffer from obesity.

Then I got MS. And there was blowback from that. At least one part wondered, did any of that matter? I'm still going to end up like my parents. The parts that internalized all of the shame and all of the identity around weight took control again, and I gained back all the weight I'd lost during training. Here I was right back at the beginning of the cycle again. I'd outrun them for years, but now I needed to dig in further to what was really underneath my weight issues.

Sugar as Emotional Companion

As I dug deeper, I found another layer—the one that linked comfort and emotional support with sugar. Imagine a baby who's crying because of colic—who's also emotionally neglected with a misattuned mother. Rather than being nurtured and comforted, I was fed Karo syrup. Now, I have a nervous system wired like one of Pavlov's dogs. Sugar = warmth and comfort. In addition to it being an emotional crutch in place of love, it was also imprinted in my nervous system.

Fighting Fires

Finally, after discovering IFS, I discovered my trusty and quite effective Firefighter—the one who comes in and douses the pain and the shame with food. It isn't just about love. It isn't about the loneliness. It's about the nervous system activation of my core wounds. And if there's anything the text in this book shows, it's that I have plenty of core wounds to choose from: a never-ending supply of kindling for raging fires.

FROM SHAME TO COMPASSION

"This Is Me"
—Kesha, from "The Greatest Showman"

A declaration of self-acceptance, embracing scars and differences unapologetically.

When I look at the many layers of my relationship to food and sugar, it's no wonder it has been a life-long struggle. It is through the lens of IFS that has allowed me to separate fully from the weight and see myself for who I really am.

I am a deeply human, deeply wounded person who has spent a lifetime battling demons that I didn't even know existed. And now that Self energy is coming back online, there is so much more grace and compassion in the system.

Not that the Inner Critic doesn't still bark. In fact, it gets quite loud at times. But I am able to return to Self. And while I allow the Critic to speak, I don't listen as much anymore. I still struggle with my weight. My Firefighter is still raging. I'm diving deep into the core wounds that the Firefighter is working so hard to protect me from. It's no wonder that my eating patterns are actually worse right now than normal. But I am giving myself grace.

I know that the only way to get to the bottom of my weight and correct it once and for all, the only way to do it, is to unburden the exiles who are creating fires.

Maybe someday I'll be in a different body. But even if I'm not, I'll be in a different *relationship* with that body. And that alone would be revolutionary.

CHAPTER THIRTEEN

The Eternal Dance of Jekyll and Hyde—Who's in Charge Today?

THE SPIRAL NOT THE LINE

"Hi Ren."
—Ren

An intimate dialogue between light and shadow, showing their eternal dance.

Every time I think I have outrun something from my past, it comes back. I used to say, "I thought I had dealt with that issue already." When my patterns resurface, my Historian and my Skeptic team up to remind me that I haven't changed after all.

I have revisited core issues on multiple occasions now, but what I have realized is that each time I do, I see them from a slightly different perspective. There are many layers to my wounds, and each time I go in, I alchemize a layer. And *that* is progress. That is change. No matter how many times I revisit something, there is always a slightly elevated awareness around it. There is always something new to learn from it.

Healing isn't a straight line. It is a spiral staircase that gradually ascends each time I revisit a problem.

The Part Party

I can go from hopeful, even joyful, to despair in a very short period of time—sometimes with seemingly little reason. That back and forth isn't a backward progression in healing. It is simply me losing Self energy from time to time and allowing a part to step in and lead. It might be a minor trigger, like some-one forgetting to return a phone call, and all of a sudden my sugar cravings are raging as my Firefighter rushes to the scene. Or, maybe my workday was overwhelming, and the Manager part that wants to pull me out of the body and into space comes calling. Or my suicide Firefighter picks up on a distress signal from somewhere in my system and rushes in with a sug-gestion. Thankfully, my Guardian part is never far away.

Healing is not only nonlinear, but it can also be unpre-dictable and at times even volatile. I learned this early in my experience with trauma/ketamine therapy. In an email to Ashley I wrote:

> How can I feel more hopeful than ever that maybe I'll finally outrun my demons yet at the same time feel the most despair and desire to just stop existing that I can remember? I have no choice but to keep moving forward because there is no going back to the simple days of being unaware.

Did you notice that both my suicide Firefighter part *and* my Guardian part voices are both in that short paragraph?

That email was prompted by some work I had done as I was reading Pete Walker's cPTSD book on grieving. He discusses the need to grieve things stolen by neglect but also advises that taming the inner critic needs to happen first. I learned the hard way when an attempt at grieving spiraled into an inner critic field day.

I went on to write:

Despite feeling pretty shitty right now, I am also quite happy with some things I put together from some flashbacks over the last several days. I got through the sections on grieving and the inner critic. I realized how grieving is out of a place of compassion, but when I try to feel emotion and move it, I still have a considerable critic component that hijacks it. And that is why it feels to me like this idea of grieving isn't helpful. Not yet anyway.

Trying to do so this weekend actually made things worse and spiraled me into passive suicidality. I get what happened, and it makes so much sense now. I have shrunk my Critic in areas, but there are a lot of hidden ones where it is still active.

Lastly, I closed with this:

Having said all of that, I know I am learning, and I will continue to grow in what feels like a very volatile and nonlinear progression. I am also starting to wipe away the denial around just how dysfunctional I am and that I need help. That, in and of itself, is enough to keep my Critic busy. I am trying to separate "I have a problem that wasn't my fault, and I need help" from "I am a huge defective mess." And separating "I know what I am facing, and I will get better" from "It's so bad it's hopeless." Fun times.

In this email I sum up why it is so easy to go back and forth between feeling hopeful and feeling despair. There is very little Self in that writing. The Guardian is talking about the Critic, the suicide Firefighter, and even referencing the wounded parts in the neglect.

My system is dynamic and complex, with many parts all

having roles that can conflict with each other in extreme fash-ion. Healing isn't getting rid of a part so that it never speaks out again. Healing is loving that part into a softer role. In the meantime, parts will be active and sometimes loud. Over time, the system hijacks are less frequent, less intense, and shorter in duration. It doesn't mean they don't ever happen. And when they do, it can feel like nothing has really changed at all. Emo-tional flashbacks can take me right back into the wound. Hon-estly, I think I will always have moments where one of my parts takes over and I pull a Jekyll and Hyde act. I call it emotional whiplash.

I am human. I am wounded. And so are my parts. But re-lating to my parts better with Self leadership, one moment at a time, is the real healing. And the moments in between? If you don't want to dance with the song right now, give it time and it will change.

PART IV

The Search for Self

CHAPTER FOURTEEN

The Chameleon and the Void

"What's It Gonna Take"
—Sarah McLachlan

A yearning question: what will it take to finally feel worthy and strong?

Who Am I?

If you'd asked me a few years ago who I was, I would've given you a resume . . . or maybe a calorie count. I didn't know myself. I only knew who I thought I needed to be to survive the moment I was in. I spent most of my life wanting to be someone—*anyone*—other than myself. I bounced from thing to thing, always identifying someone I'd rather be.

At some point I realized the "fakeness," and I developed this desire to be *authentic* and real. What was authentic and real? Who am I? I set out to discover the answers to this question. When I realized I couldn't ever answer it, because I simply didn't know who I was, I was beyond frustrated.

In all the seasons of my life where I thought I knew who I

was, I identified with the weather. As a kid and even into college, I was a softball player. Until the back injury pulled the rug of identity out from under me. Same thing with Ironman.

I didn't realize it at the time, but in those activities, I was filling a void that was created when Self energy pulled away at such an early age. So I never developed a real sense of identity. Not a healthy one anyway. Whatever identity I did have was defined by a raging Inner Critic, and "I'm fat" became the default. But the shame and guilt underneath everything was too much to sit with, and so dissociation would pull me into a void. Into the nothingness at my core.

Not only did I identify with the sport I was doing, but I also lacked boundaries—another symptom of my neglect and abuse. I spent years blending with other people so much that I got lost in them, and my identity shifted to theirs. I always knew that I identified with other people a little too much, but I couldn't ever really put my finger on it.

I have used the term "chameleon" to describe myself on multiple occasions, meaning I morphed into whoever I needed or wanted to be in any given moment depending on what I was doing or who I was with. When you don't have a sense of identity, you have to constantly create one. For me, it happened quickly and often.

Unaware of the dynamic at the time, I attached to my life and triathlon coach, Jess. Not only did I emotionally attach to her too much, I blended with her. I shaped my very identity on coaching with her and the things I was accomplishing during that time. After my Ironman race, I think we both realized that the boundaries had become blurred, and Jess began to pull back from the "friend" zone.

It was a rupture unlike anything I had ever experienced. I also sensed the overidentification and was contemplating not coaching with her for the first time in five years. In the midst of that heartache, sitting right within my core wound of neglect, I sent Jess an email about what was surfacing for me around the coaching and moving forward.

Here is an excerpt from that email that perfectly describes how my very identity had become defined by Jess and my experience with her:

January 2020

…Added to all this is also this idea of identity. My new self is less than 4 years old. It has known nothing other than coaching with you. In a way, part of my identity of the new growing Kim is framed by your coaching. What does this new Kim look like on her own? And so far, the non-coached Kim looks a lot more like her old one.

That makes me wonder how much of my growth was not only framed by your coaching but also filtered and that it isn't real; that it is "pseudo real," in that it's real as long as I am identifying myself through the coaching filter. And so maybe there is a need to step aside from coaching—from ALL coaching. And solidify my identity as just Kim, the new Kim. Not new Kim and her coach, and with any luck, not old Kim again.

Later in that email I would go on to add:

Who the fuck am I, where the fuck am I going, and how the fuck am I getting there, because nothing feels real right now.

Sadly, after Ironman and the rupture with Jess, I lost all sense of the identity I had developed, and the void enveloped me again, right back into a spiral of depression. The numbness and freeze took over, and I ended up falling right back into the "old identity of Kim." Up to that point, the Kim that existed when I wasn't identifying with something outside of me was a raging sense of emptiness. That emptiness and the stories from within it once again became the predominant identity.

At my worst I was so enmeshed with another that I couldn't tell where they ended and I began. But even in relationships and moments where I was able to maintain a bit of energetic separation, I was still making inauthentic choices. I was still deferring, shape-shifting, and calculating my words and behavior to maintain connection—because somewhere deep down, I believed that authenticity would cost me connection.

I didn't realize it at the time, but I was suppressing my authentic self for the sake of maintaining connection with others—a pattern I developed at an early age due to the neglect and abuse.

Gabor Maté puts it this way in *When the Body Says No*:

The child's attachment drive, being the stronger of the two instincts, often overrides authenticity. To maintain the relationship, the child represses self-expression.

For me, this suppression became a way of life. Even when I thought I was making independent decisions, I was often still performing. I was still scanning the emotional field of the other person and adjusting accordingly. I had internalized the idea that I couldn't be real and be loved at the same time. So I chose attachment. Again and again.

About two years after the breakup with Jess, I was dealing with my parents' declining health and the MS. I tried to write my way out of it with the proprioceptive writing. Here is another of those writings that goes to the core of that fleeting sense of identity:

3/6/22 – 3rd Write

I have spent a lot of life wanting to be someone besides myself.

I'm like a chameleon.

What do I mean by chameleon?

I change to adapt to my surroundings and people—but it's about wanting to change into someone else.

Who else? Michelle, Sharyn, Jess, etc.

Blank again—why do I not want to be myself?

I don't know, other than just not liking who I am?

There is such a discomfort in my own skin—why is that?

I don't even know what I am saying here.

I had indeed become a chameleon over the years, and I was very good at it. Often, I was able to thrive in whatever identity I had assumed. But when that identity fell apart, I spiraled. It was an up-and-down pattern that was all too familiar.

Shortly after I wrote that, I started therapy with Ashley. And I began to repeat the same pattern: overly identifying with her. However, as I mentioned earlier, she was good at gently holding boundaries for me that I had never had before. While it did trigger me initially at times, looking back I see how vital this was to my growth. Rather than identifying myself within Ashley as my therapist, I had to learn how to identify myself as someone in therapy but separate from it—and her.

That was a hard thing to do. I needed something outside of myself to identify with. So I shifted that identity into "healing." That allowed me to keep a proper distance from Ashley but still keep my identity outside of where it really needed to be: inside my Self. I think it was a necessary step because it did pull me out of the spiral and turned my energy toward the evolution I am in now. It did not, however, answer the question I started with all those years ago: "Who am I?"

In fact, therapy actually made my confusion about identity even worse. Let me explain.

As I learned about neglect and dissociation and put together the pieces around merging with others, I started to question whether *anything* in my life had been real and authentic.

I always thought I loved softball, but did I really love it? Or was it just something that made me feel good because it wasn't the void? Even though I knew I had overidentified with Jess, I did have a sense that doing the Ironman WAS authentic because it made me feel so alive. Was that fake?

I now had even less of a sense of identity than I had when I started. The other thing, though, was that years ago if someone asked me to describe myself (other than fat, which was the first thing I always thought), I would say things like "kind, generous, funny."

But through the trauma lens, after meeting Manager parts that used people-pleasing and humor to avoid pain, I began to wonder if any of it had ever been real. I spent a lot of time sinking into that, and it did not feel good. I also developed a fear that the ketamine sessions would uncover the fact that there was nothing at my core. In a proprioceptive writing shortly after my second ketamine session, I wrote:

11/7/2022

Somehow there is a fear maybe that there really isn't an identity underneath—no sense of self.

Early ketamine sessions provided a space between the old identity and the new one.

Over time, as Self energy grew through medicine sessions and therapy, I began to feel less of a void, and qualities of Self began to bleed through. It had become a bit easier to not have to have a sport, goal, or project to shape my identity.

In IFS, there are eight qualities associated with Self that represent the core essence of a person. They're called the Eight Cs of Self: calmness, curiosity, clarity, compassion, confidence, courage, connectedness, and creativity. For me, creativity had always been there, but when I am in survival mode, it isn't accessible. There simply isn't energy for it.

As I have shifted more and more into Self energy, not only do I now understand that I am indeed funny, generous, and kind, but I also genuinely love music and writing. And as I have more and more moments outside of survival mode, I am finding the energy to express qualities that were always there. But I can also separate myself from them. My sense of identity doesn't come from writing this book or singing songs. My sense of identity is Self. At the moment, my Self is being creative.

Here is a journal writing from a bit later in my progression of exploring identity through the early lens of IFS and cPTSD:

WHO AM I? In my early adult years and even in my preteen and teen years, if someone asked me, "Who are you?" I would have answered with who my Inner Critic and shame-filled parts said I was. "I am fat and ugly." The subconscious identity being "I am unlovable." I never even thought twice about it not being the authentic truth of who I was.

As I progressed in life, I added a few things to that list. I am a radiologist. I am my parents' daughter/caretaker. I do this or that. None of these things even come close to the truth of my true self—especially while maintaining "unlovable" at the center of my identity.

I never understood why I thought and felt that way and never even thought to question it. I simply was that. As I have become more aware of this idea of childhood emotional neglect and CPTSD, I see very clearly how and why I developed this really hurtful sense of self. Having spent 50 years with that identity in mind, it has without a doubt altered the course of what life may have been like with normal parental love and development. There is no going back. Only forward, and now with this awareness there is a renewed interest in this question of identity. I am realizing that there is a different true answer than what I have carried with me most of my life.

One of the hallmarks of CPTSD is a poor sense of self. I can relate. Now, as I look back at my life, I see how I have been a chameleon, changing to fit in, oftentimes connecting with a person or group that I connected with and aligning myself with their interests as if they were my own. I would actually, deep down somewhere, want to BE that person. I wanted to be anyone but myself, really.

I am not sure if that was born of my sense of self being filled with shame and self-disgust or if there was an emptiness that I was trying to fill. Regardless, I see how often I was just trying to be someone else. Now, though, as I see through this pattern and have a deep desire to really just be me, I am stuck with this question—WHO AM I?

If I am not all those things I used to think, and I am not all the people/things I have morphed into over the years, then who exactly am I? I feel like my true self has never really been in there. There is a growing desire to be authentically me. Yet I don't know how. I don't know what authentic me is. What is it even like to be me? From this place, I contemplate the meaning of "self." I have been looking for myself from an ego perspective. What do I want? Where do I want to live? What do I enjoy doing? What is my passion? My purpose? What is my ideal partner? Etc. I didn't find any answers in these questions. The "self" isn't an ego thing evidently.

The next evolution is what Richard Schwartz calls the "Self" with a capital S. An inner self that every person has, which has specific characteristics. Those are admirable qualities, and I believe in them. But creativity is broad. What is MY creativity? At this level, the 8 Cs—aren't we all the same? How am I unique? So while this idea of "Self" and the mentioned qualities is a great start, it feels incomplete to me in defining my personal authentic self.

Reflecting back on that writing, I was starting to understand that Self was at the core of identity, but I still had some confusion as to what made me unique. If Self is universal, then what makes me Kim?

That answer would come later during a medicine session.

I was spending a lot of time in my Comedian part, joking about the pain of the ketamine injection, and I referenced a song. Ashley thought I was bringing in a different part, but what came up was that I was still in the Comedian but that another part had *helped* the Comedian by providing a musical reference. I noticed how there was a sense of collaboration among my parts. For a long time, I thought each part acted alone. But in that session, I watched them work together, like a symphony tuning itself. The Comedian delivered the punchline, but it was the Musician who handed her the mic. Here is an excerpt from my journal writing after that ketamine session:

> . . . There is something important in the "my parts are collaborating" thing that came up. When asking the questions "What is real?" and "What do I like?" or "What gives me joy?", I claim to not know myself or that I'm being inauthentic. But the truth is, these Manager parts are tapping into other parts for help. These Manager parts KNOW me and how to communicate to me in a language that IS real and authentic. The Musician part and the Comedian part —those parts are REAL qualities that the Managers use to communicate. And I can start to separate the managing from the quality and understand that the quality is ME."

"The quality is ME." All along, I hadn't been trying to create a new identity out of nothing. I was simply trying to rediscover, and believe in, the things that were already there in my parts.

My parts were me. And they were starting to function as a family unit rather than a bunch of fragmented runaways.

I had a profound realization that the real me was in there all along—that my parts and the qualities they possess ARE in fact real. The maladaptive response wasn't to create fake qualities; it merely took real ones and exaggerated them.

ANSWERING THE QUESTION

"Who I Am"
—Wyn Starks

A triumphant declaration of authenticity, finally stepping fully into selfhood.

Circling back to "Who am I?" I can finally, after years of searching, answer it. I am Self. I am Calm, Curiosity, Compassion, Clarity, Confidence, Courage, Creativity, and Connected.

But I am also my parts, and they possess some cool qualities. I am the intelligence of my Analyzer part. I am the humor of my Comedian. I am the tenderness of my Exiles. I am the collection of stories and experiences as stored in my Historian. I am the struggle and the effort—but also the unwavering persistence and resilience of my Guardian. I am a bit skeptical thanks to my Skeptic. I am even the parts that love food. I am all of these things.

At times, the parts work in harmony and create this sense of wholeness that is ME. I still have plenty of times where a Firefighter or a Manager tips the balance and I find myself in old patterns. With a strong foundation in my sense of Self, however, I can face it with grace and compassion until Self returns.

"Survive"
—Lewis Capaldi

*A cry of determination: even through pain,
there's still something left to give.*

Career: From Surviving to Writing

I first entered medical school, inspired by numerous sports injuries, with aspirations of sports medicine. Looking back, I see how medicine was a choice from the head, not from the heart—driven by achievement and proving worth.

Early on in my training I realized I wasn't a people person and I lacked the confidence needed to be a surgeon. Thus, orthopedics/sports medicine fell away. The question then became, what now? After a rotation in radiology, I had a new direction. I was drawn to it because I didn't have to interact with patients much. It was a perfect choice for who I was at the time: emotionally shut down, relationally challenged, and carrying a great deal of shame. Radiology allowed me to hide within medicine. It served me well for years.

What does a radiologist do? In short, I interpret medical imaging. CT scans, MRIs, x-rays, ultrasounds, and more. Most of my day is spent in front of a computer dictating reports. There is little interaction with others. As I have evolved, I realize that radiology is not my soul calling. Not even close. I am much more of a people person than I used to be. I now desire connection where I used to run from it. And I have more confidence.

I chose my career by the age of sixteen, more out of survival than vocation. I was a chameleon even in career choice. Would I go back and change things if I could? Most definitely. Maybe I would be a musician. A teacher. Not sure, but definitely not a radiologist. Without my experiences as a doctor, could I be a writer?

Writing, I think, is my soul calling. Radiology let me hide. Writing now allows me to be seen.

But radiology has also been good to me. I have a steady and high income that's allowed me to pursue experiences many can't. Hundreds of sporting events and concerts. Travel. Coaching, including for an Ironman. I have always been able to do whatever I wanted to do financially. Looking back, though, I see how much of those pursuits were attempts to fill the void born out of emotional neglect and abuse.

And while they may have temporarily managed the void, none of those things ever did fill it. The thing that helped the most cost nothing: sitting with myself. I had to stop running to get anywhere.

Now, that income has allowed me to do ketamine therapy regularly. I am blessed in that regard.

The irony is that being a radiologist doesn't fit the person I am anymore. But I would not be the person I am now without it. Nothing is wasted, not even a misaligned career choice.

# CHAPTER FIFTEEN

Home Is a Song

"Home Is a Song"
—Mary Chapin Carpenter

*The reminder that home is not a place,
but a feeling carried in music.*

A LOVE IS BORN

"I've Got the Music in Me"
—Heart

I have always loved music. It is so much a part of who I am that I couldn't write a book about my journey and *not* devote some pages to it. I don't recall exactly when it landed for me, but as you may remember, I sang in a talent show at a young age. When I was in grade school, I listened to Billy Joel's *An Innocent Man* album on repeat. I was drawn to the tenor saxophone sound on the song "This Night," and once I was old enough for school band, I decided to take up this instrument.

I played saxophone through high school, in the symphonic band and in marching and jazz bands. I had some sort of music class during four of my school hours during my senior year in high school. I was a good saxophone player and could play music off a score with technical skill, but I was never quite able to connect with the music in an expressive and creative way. In jazz, it is common to play solos where you are given only the chord changes; you play from the heart in an unwritten and unscripted manner. This is called improvisation, and I wasn't very good at it.

Before I had words for trauma and dissociation, I froze whenever it came time for my solo in jazz class.

I wasn't bad at improvisation because I lacked talent. *I was bad at it because I lacked safety.*

Survival mode and creativity cannot coexist. I was playing music from my head, not my heart.

THE GIRL AND THE JAZZ MAN: CHAMELEON REVISITED

"Chameleon"
—Herbie Hancock

A playful, shifting jazz piece reflecting adaptability and change.

The highlight of my school music career was meeting and playing next to Branford Marsalis. He was the featured artist at the Wichita Jazz Festival my senior year, and he did a clinic with our jazz band. We played a Herbie Hancock tune for him, and when we finished, he just shook his head.

"Play that again," he said, unpacking his beautiful shiny tenor saxophone from its case. I was playing first tenor at the time, and he stood next to me and read off my sheet music while we played that song again. He was a jazz legend; I'll never forget that moment. Oh, the song we played? It was titled "Chameleon."

When I went to college, I tucked my saxophone away in a

case to collect dust while I studied and partied. But while I wasn't playing music, I did continue to love it. And as I matured into a college and then medical student, music became a form of soul communication.

I listened to a wide variety of music—always dependent on my emotional state. I couldn't truly feel or express emotion, but I could always find a song that spoke for me. Some songs did it musically—the drumbeat or guitar lick hit something deep inside. With other songs, it was the lyrics—words that described how I was feeling that often went deeper than my understanding at the time, but my soul knew they were right.

Music wasn't merely a way I connected to myself; it became a way to connect with others. I share songs with people a *lot*. One look at the playlist from this book and you get the idea. I communicate through music.

For the longest time, if I shared a song with someone and they didn't get it or like it, it would be a paper cut to my psyche. Why? It wasn't just a song I was sharing—I was sharing a part of me. And it was a subtle form of rejection that went right into that core of shame.

I didn't understand the dynamic until I started working on self-awareness and realized what was happening. I still share songs as a way to share part of me, but I don't internalize shame when someone rejects one. So if you don't like a song in my book soundtrack, I'm totally cool with that. Find your own groove. But at least you took the time to listen.

Over the years, I tried many times to return to music. I took piano and guitar lessons, neither for very long. Life would get in the way, and I would rarely practice between lessons, so the skill would fizzle out before I ever got anywhere.

I have long dreamt of being able to play guitar and/or piano, but my trauma surfaced here as well: I couldn't stick with it when it felt hard. I would give up rather than work through. I'm not sure if it was the shame of not being very good, the frustration of the Guardian part who wants to be good from the first moment, or a protector saving me from disappointment, but there were parts of me that quit on music many times. This was a case of internal conflict for sure. I had the Musician part wanting to express itself. I had parts that didn't want to practice and the part that got frustrated with the process. But I also had the Inner Critic calling me lazy and undisciplined when I didn't practice.

I learned that poor self-discipline is a feature of emotional neglect. Reparenting myself was not only going to have to include maternal nurturing but also some paternal discipline.

Looking back, I see how I was trying to force music into a life that was 110 percent survival mode. That could never work.

SINGING FOR MOM

"Scars in Heaven"
—Casting Crowns

*A vision of loved ones free from suffering,
bringing comfort in grief.*

Shortly after the Ironman, I had lost the high and started searching for the next thing. I returned to music. Instead of unpacking my saxophone, though, I took up voice lessons. I had never sung in any formal setting. My experience with singing was belting out tunes in the car or shower. I knew I had a decent voice, but it was raw.

I also knew from the self-awareness I had already obtained that I was not speaking my truth. According to several practitioners, I had a blocked throat chakra. My instincts knew they were right. So I signed up for voice lessons, not only to rekindle my love for music but also to expand my ability to express myself vocally. Now, my music lessons were more than learning to play an instrument. They were a tool for self-evolution, and that allowed me to stay in it. Little did I know at the time about the doors that would open because of this choice.

About a year or so into lessons, my mom died. I had picked out a song to play at her funeral: "Scars in Heaven" by Casting Crowns. It was a beautiful song with rich symbolism for the wounds that my mom and I shared. A few days before the service, I got the idea of singing it myself. I knew I couldn't sing it live, but I thought maybe I could record it.

In a matter of days, I found a recording studio, a sound/recording engineer (Chuck), and a guitar player (Kurt) to help me record this song. I showed up at the studio with no idea what I was going to do, but after a short collaboration, we went to work recording. After Kurt recorded his guitar track, I stepped up to the fancy microphone with headphones on. I sang the words several times through. I hit the notes, and it sounded good.

But I wasn't singing from my soul. I was holding back, because even in singing a song for my mom's funeral, I was detached from my emotion. It sounded good; it just wasn't as emotionally expressive as Chuck or I wanted. I was still making music from the head, not from the heart.

I played the song at the funeral, surprising even my closest friends and family, who had no idea I could sing. It was a fitting and symbolic gesture. My dad had passed before my mother, and I was now in an "orphaned" state. I felt a release from the energetic blending I had with my parents my entire life, and I chose music as a way to tell the world that I was no longer my parents' daughter. I was going to be Kim now.

SCARS IN HEAVEN
https://bit.ly/KT-Scars-in-Heaven

SINGING FOR ME: BIRD SET FREE

"Bird Set Free"
—*Sia*

A release of shame and fear, claiming the freedom to sing one's truth.

Even though it was for a sad occasion, I tapped into a soul joy. Mom's funeral was in February 2023. I moved on from her death and re-engaged in normal life, but I couldn't move on from how much I enjoyed recording the song.

That November I had an idea: I was going to record a Christmas song and send it to friends and family as a musical Christmas card. I had a song in mind and knew exactly what I wanted to do. The song was "'Til the Season Comes 'Round Again."

YouTube — All Videos Playlist

https://bit.ly/Till-the-Season-Comes-Round-Again

The version I was familiar with was by Amy Grant. I contacted Chuck and asked him to help me again.

Before I knew it, I was back in the recording studio with

Chuck and Kurt. I also now had a piano player and a second vocalist singing harmony, my good friend Jo. I hired a videographer to record the day, and I made a music video to the track from the footage and sent out a YouTube link that Christmas. I was in the flow. There was joy in my heart the entire time.

Then I did it again the next year; this time, the song was "Christmas in Heaven."

https://bit.ly/Christmas-in-Heaven

I am now in the process of recording an entire album. My goal is to take my writing skill and love for music and eventually write some original stuff. For now, I am having the time of my life making music with Chuck, who has become a good friend. He has his own journey through trauma and truly gets why the music is so important to me. It isn't just a hobby. It is soul-level expression. While I am still evolving to be more expressive and heartfelt in my music, the creative process is fuel for the soul.

Now, through my work with IFS, I have met my Musician part. He has surfaced many times during ketamine sessions, sometimes effortlessly offering up a musical selection and sometimes sending the musical reference to another part. And in coming home to the identity of Self and my parts, I have fully accepted that music is in the very fabric of my being. It is the very definition of authentic expression I was looking so hard for years ago. It was there all along. The girl who sang "Maybe" at that talent show knew it.

No matter what life brings or where I find myself, I can always find home in a song and myself in the melody.

CHAPTER SIXTEEN

Bring On the Wonder—
The Search for Spirituality

A plea to bring back the soul's hidden wonder after too much silence.

Cerebral Seeking

Religion is one of the first things I turned to years ago when I first heard the faint call that there was something more to life than oscillating between okay and major depression. I was raised as a nonpracticing, in-name-only Christian. My parents didn't go to church, and neither did I. I did go to Sunday School for a while in junior high, but that was more for the social aspect. I never even thought about what it meant to be a Christian, and I certainly never felt any sort of connection to God. For years—through college, medical school, and residency—I didn't give religion or God a second thought.

During a major depressive episode early in my medical

practice, I turned back toward the religion I inherited—and I went all in. I attended church regularly. I read the Bible. I went to Bible study, and I even bought a collection of Joyce Meyer books and tapes. It didn't help. While it gave me something to focus on and temporarily lifted my outlook, the deeper connection I was craving never came. It was purely a cerebral practice.

After I started working with Jess, my former life and Ironman coach, I started questioning things more critically, including my religion. What did it mean to be a Christian, and what exactly did I believe? It was very dualistic: I was separate from God. And the Christian teaching that we are inherently sinners by our very nature was shaming. It could certainly throw gasoline on a pre-existing fire of shame. I also struggled with the idea that Christianity was the only way to God.

I started reading other texts. In particular, I was drawn to Buddhist teachings. But I was still confused. What did I really believe?

Then I read *Without Buddha I Could Not Be a Christian* by Paul Knitter. In it, he outlined the issues he had with Christian doctrine, explored that issue from a Buddhist perspective, and then reconciled the two into a new understanding. I sent Jess an email with my thoughts and insights as I read through the book. Here is an excerpt from that email that shows just how cerebral I was in my approach to God:

2017

As for the spiritual thoughts/compassion arena, I am really deep into this book on being a "Buddhist Christian." It's a game changer.
In my black-and-white world view (and a lot of Christianity is black and white), I've seen things

through that standard Christianity lens. And this guy makes the point that we've gotten to where we are too defined and literal in our thoughts on the Divine. That our problem is not a lack of meaning but an excess of it—ignoring the possibility of meaning in lieu of determination of meaning. That puts big shackles on a divine that is supposed to be mysterious and, in a lot of ways, unknown. There is a need to get back to the mystery of the Divine.

Another area that is really hitting home is in this black-and-white, literal Christian doctrine world. The "truths" in Christian doctrine have become barriers to exploring deeper content. It sets up walls that limit not only exploring alternate ideology within Christianity but also ideas outside of Christianity.

Christian truth can be destructive toward other truths. And within the mystery of the Divine, we cannot possibly even begin to understand everything about God.

The Christian church has a lot of "one-and-only"-type language that this author claims we should be wary of. He also talks about how rather than viewing God as a person, it should be felt as personal. It's an experience, not a doctrine. And I tend to agree with that—but the doctrine can get in the way.

In a lot of ways, for some reason, reading this book is really just an attempt to connect with a true divine experience. Not that I haven't had spiritual connection at times, but a true feeling of connectedness with it and through me is lacking—and that's why I think this mental shift in focusing on more compassion and awareness is coming into major play.

It may be that I don't really need to change much about my life at all in terms of what I do and what I have—job, where I live, etc.—I just needed to change me.

My spirituality was shifting from the idea of a single God with rules to the idea of God in everything, manifest through compassion, and although I don't explicitly say it, love. This was the beginning of a shift that wouldn't fully happen until years later.

At the end of the book, Knitter commented that he didn't know if he was a Buddhist Christian or a Christian Buddhist. That raised a similar question for me. What was I? In the same email I sent Jess, I go on to ponder that very question:

> The question becomes, though, by deconstructing these written words of religion and putting shades of gray on the very core of Christian 'belief'—how far can you go before it's no longer 'Christianity' but some variant or unrecognizable set of beliefs? I can say wholeheartedly I am not Buddhist. That much I can say. I still define myself as a Christian—and as he describes, if there are fragments you hang onto that point you to the moon (God), then it is still a worthwhile concept. I think that is where I am—definitely Christian but fragmented. Just trying to figure out how far I will end up going on the spectrum and what the end "product" looks like.

I still remember Jess's simple yet profound response to my confusion about my religious identity: "I'm curious about the necessity to label spirituality . . ." It was an aha moment. I *didn't* need to have a label.

STILL DISCONNECTED, STILL CEREBRAL: JUST DIFFERENT

"Eden"
—Sarah Bareilles

A song about innocence lost and the painful aftermath of deception.

I eventually discovered Joe Dispenza and his quantum physics-based approach to spirituality. He used terms like "divine," "light," and "energy" together in a scientific way that my head could wrap around. His cerebral approach to spirituality felt like it was custom-made for me. That was the beginning of a long period where I explored more New Age practices.

I meditated with Joe Dispenza. I dabbled in Reiki treatments. I branched off into some Eastern practices—including chanting and breath work—all in an attempt to connect with something that felt spiritual. I had a few fleeting moments, but ultimately, I didn't feel any more spiritual in my New Age cape than I did quoting my Bible.

What the New Age approach did do, though, was encourage my already strong hyper-independence. The non-dualistic idea of being divine within negated any sense of need for anything outside of me. Looking back, it's no wonder I didn't feel any spiritual connection. In some ways, my New Age modalities took me further away from it. I also didn't develop any more compassion or love; I merely shifted my cerebral focus from God outside of me to God within me. But my connection to God and to myself was still largely absent.

Trauma and God

As I worked with Ashley and psychedelics, I understood that my disconnection from God was also a result of my hijacked nervous system.

Some people seem to have faith easily. They pray, they trust, and they feel connected to something greater—almost instinctively. I used to think there was something wrong with me because I couldn't do that. I blamed myself for not having enough faith.

But now I understand. It wasn't a lack of faith. It was a lack of safety. When you've lived through trauma, God can feel like just another place you might be abandoned.

As I started the ketamine sessions, I was not only hoping to heal the MS by excavating and releasing emotion, but I was also hoping that I would finally feel something spiritual. I had listened to podcasts, read stories, and entertained firsthand accounts of deeply spiritual and mystical experiences during psychedelic encounters with the divine. As I thought about having a similar experience, I realized that ironically, I was also afraid of it. I thought maybe that was why I couldn't connect: because deep down I was afraid.

Despite my fear, I stayed open to the desire for a spiritual experience. Surely, I thought, the medicine sessions would give me a spiritual connection. Initially, the ketamine failed to induce anything close to a spiritual experience. Over time, though, I started having glimpses of something divine, although it was not the in-your-face mystical moment many people describe. My experience was more of a slow build. Moments of feeling something more expansive than myself here and there. Thoughts and images of Jesus or Moses. Messages that clearly weren't coming from me, although at times I wasn't sure if it was my Self energy or something outside of me. All I know is they seemed different than my normal thoughts.

One ketamine session moment stuck with me. I got a message that what's blocking my connection to God is pride. I realized that my pride, and more specifically, my hyper-independence and refusal to ask for help, was what was behind the block. While I was focused on fear, I was missing the big picture. I broke down in tears. Finally, a real moment with a real message.

I simply needed to drop the defenses and ask for help with that connection. Yet, after leaving Ashley's office that day, asking was still a thing I struggled with.

I also had moments in the ketamine sessions where I flashed anger at God. During one ketamine journey, as I was feeling the somatic discomfort of trauma in my legs, I had a vision of my heart actually flowing out of my chest.

Ashley asked me where it went. Could I see it? I answered, "No, where is my heart?!"

YouTube — All Ketamine Sessions Playlist

VIDEO CLIP 8
https://bit.ly/KT-Ketamine-Session-Clip8

A bit later in the session, I saw myself trying to connect with God. God was looking down at my heartless chest rather than my heart, which was floating elsewhere. He wasn't helping me find my heart; he was waiting for me to find him without one. Later, Ashley asked me how I felt about God and what I saw.

VIDEO CLIP 9
https://bit.ly/KT-Ketamine-Session-Clip9

As I answered her, I realized how angry I was at God. I said, "God says that you have to seek him. Seek and you shall find . . . yet, when someone is so walled off from trauma that they don't know how to seek, you leave them on their own to find you!"

"How about you reach down and help me out?!" I sobbed.

VIDEO CLIP 10
https://bit.ly/KT-Ketamine-Session-Clip10

When I take a step back from all the fear, pride, and anger that was in my way, I can see that God *has* been reaching down to help: the moments of awareness, the people who cross my path, the perfect timing of opportunities, etc.—all of it is assistance that all along was leading me here.

Discovering Ashley when I did was some sort of divine intervention. Mindy, my psilocybin guide, was also a synchronous encounter that has resulted in a beautiful addition to my support team. There have also been more subtle nudges that ultimately end up leading me to the right decisions. In the past, I might not have noticed the nudges.

It had become clear that even though I may not fully believe Christian doctrine in its current form, my spiritual connection existed through Jesus. Images of Jesus appeared during some of my sessions with a level of familiarity that felt right. However, what I am learning is that the absolute views of the Christian Church are too dualistic and shaming for me. New Age is too independent. The spirituality I seek is somewhere in the middle.

There is something to recognizing and honoring the fact that we are inherently divine. The Bible says we're made in God's image, after all. There is also something to surrendering to something greater than yourself.

I have come full circle, and as I settle in on what my beliefs and spiritual needs are, I am moving toward cultivating connection. It is still faint, but it has a heartbeat. I am in the process of developing a spiritual life. What does that look like?

Well, I still struggle with being too independent and not thinking to ask.

SEEDS OF SURRENDER

"Kyrie"
—*Mr. Mister*

A prayer for mercy and guidance
along the path.

Recently, I met with a spiritual director to help me explore my beliefs and cultivate my spiritual life. Early on in the session, she asked me a question she asks all her new clients: "How do you feel about the state of your soul?"

As I began a long, winding answer about my healing journey, I started crying. This surprised me. Why was I so emotional? It wasn't because I was scared or sad about the state of my soul.

As I leaned in, I discovered the tears were from the joy of my soul finally coming home. At the close of our hour, she asked me how I wanted to end my session. I thought about it briefly, then answered, "I would like to end it with a prayer."

I explained that prayer had always been uncomfortable and hard for me and that it's not my first instinct. I told her how much I wanted to change that. Although I didn't say this part out loud, I knew this discomfort was due to my Skeptic being loud with the "this is bullshit" and "this is stupid" commentary.

We ended with a prayer, and she sent me home with an exercise to try: the simple gesture of closing both hands around whatever problem I was having and then opening them up, releasing the problem to Jesus.

A few days later, I was in bed for the night, and the MS symptoms in my legs were grabbing my attention. I had been pretty active that day, and I was hurting a bit more than normal. My mind started spiraling into the fear and grief around MS and what the future might bring.

Then I remembered the exercise.

I closed my hands tight around the MS. I held it for a bit, and then with all the intention I could muster, I opened my hands and released the MS to Jesus. I was surprised again to find myself sobbing. I had always imagined a dramatic moment of surrender, but that night lying in bed, I experienced a profound and subtle quiet.

Kyrie Eleison is Latin for "Lord, have mercy." I felt mercy in that moment.

Since then, rather than falling into an anxiety spiral around the MS like I normally would, I've had a softening. There has been a gentle invitation to bring in better self-care. It wasn't a big explosive thing, but there have been moments where I have a soft and tender feeling toward my body and genuinely want to treat it well. I don't think that is a coincidence.

My experience of spiritual connection in that moment was unassuming, and the results were just as much so. Those moments can be easily missed when only looking for loud bangs.

I thought I'd find God through thought. I thought He was something I had to fight for. But He was here all along—I just had to surrender.

You Know You Can Heal This

There have been a handful of moments on this journey where the universe (God) seemed to conspire in my favor—where grace cracked through the noise of fear and self-doubt, and I said yes. One of those moments came in early 2023, in Costa Rica.

Not long after I began working with Ashley—and was first introduced to IFS—I received an email from a retreat center in Costa Rica advertising a weeklong retreat on trauma. Several guest faculty were listed, and as I scanned the names, one jumped off the page: *Richard Schwartz, PhD.* I had just started learning about IFS and thought, *That would be cool.*

Then I kept reading.

Another name leapt out: *Gabor Maté, MD.*

Now the retreat wasn't just interesting. It was calling my name.

I had already read *In the Realm of Hungry Ghosts* and deeply connected to the stories of addiction, trauma, and pain that Gabor shared so openly. His other book, *When the Body Says No*, had planted the very first seed in me that emotional wounds could be at the root of illness. I was a big fan. And this retreat offered me the chance to learn from both these men—and visit Costa Rica? I signed up quickly and began counting down the days until February 2023.

But life had its own timing.

In the months leading up to the retreat, my mom's health took a sharp decline. She was entering hospice, and I became her full-time caregiver. As the date of the trip neared, it became clear her passing was imminent. I was faced with an impossible decision: stay or go.

After a couple of sleepless nights, I knew. I needed to go—for me. I kissed her goodbye, said what I needed to say, and walked out the door with my bags packed, aware that she might die while I was gone.

That choice—terrifying as it was—turned out to be divinely inspired.

Before even arriving at the retreat center, the synchronicities were obvious. I was blessed to be seated next to a wonderful member of the retreat faculty on the shuttle ride from the airport: Patti Elledge, a developmentally based somatic therapist. We talked for nearly two hours on the long ride to the retreat. She was so warm and engaging in her presence that I immediately felt safe and comfortable for the week ahead. I knew from that moment I had made the right decision.

The retreat was deeply moving. The faculty, including Dr. Schwartz, offered demonstrations of their methods. Each time, participants lined up, hoping to be selected. His method was simple but fair: he laid out a deck of playing cards, and whoever drew the highest card would be chosen.

One morning, I drew the highest card.

Excitement surged—followed almost immediately by panic. I was about to go on stage in a full room of people and have *Richard Schwartz*—who went by the nickname Dick—led me through an IFS session. My heart was racing. My palms were sweating. But I stepped forward anyway.

In minutes, Dick helped me soften some protectors, and I dropped into an exile—a baby. I began shaking. My chest felt tight, as if something was pressing down. It was overwhelming. Looking back, I recognize this as the early emergence of the "suffocating baby" that would later appear in full form during a ketamine session. It was short but powerful. I left feeling cracked open—and more hopeful than I had felt in a long time.

The next morning, Dick found me and asked how I was doing. I told him my chest felt lighter. I could breathe more easily. That was no coincidence.

But the moment that stayed with me most happened later in the week.

Gabor Maté had witnessed my session. A quiet and deeply present man, he approached me afterward and started a conversation. We chatted for a few minutes—about trauma, the body, and even psychedelics. I couldn't believe he was talking to *me*.

A few days later, he approached again. This time, he looked directly into my eyes and said, "You know you can heal this."

He didn't say it casually. His eyes were calm but piercing—like he was looking straight into me. And he meant it. He believed it.

Here was the man who wrote the book on trauma and illness. And he was telling *me* I could heal.

That moment changed me.

I came home from Costa Rica full of belief, awe, and gratitude. About forty-eight hours after I returned, my mother passed away. I didn't miss her death after all. And I didn't miss my own rebirth either.

That retreat was a turning point. Not because it cured me. But because it gave me a felt sense of what healing actually is. It's not the absence of MS or the erasure of trauma. It's the presence of Self—of trust, of love, of breath.

The week in Costa Rica didn't give me all the answers. But it gave me something even more essential: a felt sense of being held—by Self, by others, by something larger than me. When Gabor said, "You know you can heal this," I believed him. More importantly, I began to believe in myself. And that belief, that whisper of faith, became the soil from which the rest of my healing grew.

CHAPTER SEVENTEEN

The Divine and Life Purpose

"Lifesong"
—Casting Crowns

*A hope that one's life itself
becomes a song of meaning.*

As my search for divine connection was progressing, I had a parallel and equally frustrating desire to fulfill my divine purpose in life. It turns out that they weren't separate but a combined quest that ultimately required surrender.

I'd had the calling to some higher purpose that I never seemed to be able to put my finger on—other than the fact that I knew I wasn't living it. Radiology was not my soul calling, and neither were any of the identity-chasing experiments like Ironman.

I tried for years to find my calling by forcing my way into things my ego thought might be it. I confused excitement for divine inspiration and flamed out before I got anywhere.

For a while, I thought my calling might be in the alternate

wellness arena. I attended a functional medicine conference and came home convinced that that was what I was supposed to do. A few years ago, I bought a cabin with the intention of growing organic food—convinced *that* was my purpose.

I could name many more.

The point is, I endeavored for quite a long time and felt like I was beating my head against a brick wall. Sometimes I'd pause and tell myself to allow something to come. When nothing did, I would try to force something again. I repeated that cycle numerous times. I even tried on several occasions to write a book about my experiences, each time giving up before even a full chapter was on the page.

Here is an excerpt from a pre-ketamine proprioceptive writing that speaks to how I see purpose:

3/10/22

I am afraid of the end of my life being filled with regret. I have come to see the value in slowing down, etc., and I don't need to accomplish any particular thing. I have shifted my focus to self-awareness and living out my purpose. What do I mean by purpose? That I have tapped into my true soul calling and am outwardly manifesting it to the best of my ability. Sounds simple, but what is it? The desire to figure it out is driving me crazy. It's the regret of not finding my purpose that I am truly afraid of.

It is clear from this writing that I had evolved beyond allowing things like Ironman to define my life. However, I still had a need for something to fill a void. I had just shifted it to a more noble something.

After working with Ashley for several months, healing became more centered in my daily existence, and I thought that my *healing* was my purpose. That made a lot of sense. It also helped frame the overwhelming amount of trauma and struggle I had endured into something I could live with.

But some of my Manager parts were not satisfied with that: healing as a purpose wasn't nearly flashy enough. As I have progressed and have come more into Self energy, I realize that healing indeed has been my purpose all along. And I am okay with that.

I am shifting patterns—not just for me, but for my family that came before me, and I am making my own contribution to the larger cosmic shift in our world.

Now, as I have relaxed into healing being enough, I am writing profusely. My purpose is shifting from healing to healing *and* sharing. The healing is fueling the writing, and the writing is deepening my healing. I think that is one of the reasons I cried when the spiritual director asked me the question about my soul. I had finally resolved the tension I felt when I wrote about the fear of not finding my purpose. I am no longer searching for purpose; I am living it.

It was there all along. I just had to find my voice. And to do that, I had to stop the struggle. As my Self emerged and my Soul came home, I was able to. Maybe that was the point all along: not to find God, but to become someone safe enough to receive what had been reaching for me the whole time.

I'm no longer searching for a flashy calling. I'm letting my life itself be the song I sing. And that's enough.

Finding My Voice—A Divine Gift

"Unwritten"
—Natasha Bedingfield

A celebration of possibility: the future is a blank page waiting to be lived.

For years, I knew I wanted to tell my story. I also knew I could write. But all of my early attempts felt forced and inauthentic. I hadn't yet found my voice, because I wasn't writing from Self. I was writing from my Guardian at best and from other protectors at worst.

And then there was the imposter syndrome.

I didn't think my story was that unique. I certainly didn't think anyone would care to read it. That was the conflict: some parts heard the call to write, while others dismissed it. I had whispers telling me that what I had to say mattered. I had others telling me I was nothing special at all.

I hid behind that imposter syndrome for a long time.

But during a recent psilocybin journey, something shifted. The theme of the session was to stop narrating my life from the outside looking in and to start *living inside* it. To stop denying not just pain, but joy too. At one point, I heard the message clearly and said it out loud to Mindy, my therapist guide:

"This is a gift from the mushrooms. They're telling me I AM special. And that my life is not going to look like others."

That moment changed everything.

It gave me the internal permission to step fully into my story. To stop editing for safety. To start writing from Self. And this book —the one you're holding now—is the result.

PART V

Emergence

CHAPTER EIGHTEEN

The Pilot Light

"Atlas Falls"
—Shinedown

The promise that even under unbearable weight,
someone will rise to carry it.

The Depression

I didn't want to bore you with too many details at the beginning. I thought it was best to keep it short and dive right into the juicy part: the healing. But the truth is, my story of self-discovery started long before the events that precipitated my latest round of therapy. Parts of this story make more sense through a retrospective lens. I want you to see this story after the plot twist, not before.

I'll take you back to when I first started wondering if there was more to life than misery. Up until my graduation from medical school, I always had some next thing on my radar to keep my goal-oriented Managers satisfied. Graduate college, go to medical school, graduate from medical school, do a residency, pass boards, and get a job. I was driven and successful. I never had to sit with myself because I always had something else to focus on.

Then, after starting my career as a private practice radiologist, things changed. I suddenly didn't have some big next step on my agenda. This was it. Get up, go to work, go home, and go to bed, and then do it all over again. It wasn't long after I started practice before a major depression set in. My Managers were no longer satisfied and needed something to work toward, but I had no idea what.

It was then that I decided to give a triathlon a try. I wasn't a good runner, but I was an athlete, and it gave me a goal. My Manager parts were in control again. It was a short, sprint-distance race, which, in retrospect, was minimal compared to my Ironman. But it was challenging at the time and kept the depression at bay for a brief period.

Soon after, I found myself spiraling into a deep depression that culminated in drinking at the bar after work in a self-destructive stupor. If I had any propensity to becoming an alcoholic, this would have been the doorway. I went to bed every night, not actively suicidal, but wishing I could just not wake up. I didn't want to die, but I didn't want to live either—a feeling I had lived with off and on my entire life.

I had to do something, but I was too proud to admit I had a problem. I started by trying to treat myself with samples of antidepressants from the sample closet at work. Admitting you have a mental health issue is hard enough. When you are a medical professional, it's even harder. Not surprisingly, self-treatment with only medication didn't work. The depression continued to deepen, and although I was highly functioning at work, I was a complete mess at home.

Finally, my best friend at the time insisted I seek therapy. I think she got tired of my late-night despair-filled texts. As I said earlier, she practically dragged me there, and it took several sessions before I would say much of anything. But over time, therapy did manage to help lift my depression. And after a suggestion from my therapist, Melissa, I signed up for a marathon through Team in Training—a fundraiser for the Leukemia and Lymphoma Society (LLS). You raise money for the organization, and in return, they train you as a team to do an endurance event.

I signed up for a marathon in San Francisco, which I ran in October of 2010. While grueling, training for and doing that event made me feel alive again. Not only were my goal-oriented Managers happy again, but I was part of a community, and for that brief time, I didn't feel as lonely.

So that next summer, I signed up for another event. This time it was a 100-mile bike ride around Lake Tahoe. I had an amazing experience, and to this day, crossing the finish line of that challenging bike ride is a highlight of my life. I was hooked. I remembered that early short triathlon I had done and decided to sign up for another one, this time with LLS. It was while training for that event that I met Sharyn.

The Coach and the Spark

Sharyn was a coach for the team and was an experienced Ironman herself. She was an inspiring figure, I felt myself drawn to her right away. She also saw something in me, and after the race she approached me about working with her on my fitness and weight (which through all of this was still an issue).

I jumped at the chance, and for a three-month period, I trained at her gym twice a day several times a week. I became really fit, really fast, and dropped some weight. More importantly, though, I had a true mentor, maybe for the first time ever. Someone who saw me, cared about me, and invested in me. That sparked something inside that, at the time, I couldn't name.

Looking back, I see I attached to her from my childhood wounded parts that never had that healthy attachment growing up. It was as if she had become a surrogate mother figure to my inner child.

I thrived. I did more races. I was high on life and feeling great about myself. Although not realizing it at the time, I was borrowing off her energy and becoming lost in it. This became a pattern.

For a while, though, it kept me happy and moving forward. You might think my Ironman story is coming next, right?

Well, it would end up being another several years before I took my place at the Ironman starting line—and a whole lot of life happened in between.

The First Original Descent

Just as I was really starting to entertain the idea of doing a longer distance race, life came crashing down. I tore my Achilles tendon and required surgery.

At that same time, I took in a foster teenager at the request of another trainer/therapist who worked at Sharyn's gym.

That went poorly and, not surprisingly, added a tremendous amount of stress.

My radiology practice was also going through multiple changes, and I found myself going from being an outpatient clinic doc back to working in a hospital.

But the mother of all stressors happened on January 1, 2015.

I am standing at my kitchen sink peeling potatoes for the scalloped potatoes I'm taking to the family New Year's Day dinner that afternoon. My phone rings. Setting down the knife, I answer.

It's my brother Scott. "I'm not sure what we're going to do about dinner," he says, "but the house is in flames." He is so matter of fact and calm, so I ask him to repeat it. "The house is on fire!"

I call out to my friend from Colorado, who is still sleeping in my basement, to tell her I have to go. She emerges and offers to go with me. We rush to the car, potatoes still in the sink.

It is a long ten-minute drive to my parents' house. Desperate to get there, I detour around two large fire trucks, lights still flashing. We finally pull up in front of the neighbors' house. I throw the car in park before we even stop.

The scene is surreal. The fire is mostly out, but there is still smoke billowing from the roof. My brother is on the lawn talking to a fireman. Two news trucks are parked in the street with cameramen setting up. My parents are in the neighbors' garage, wrapped in blankets. My friend and I rush to them. I am without emotion. My parents and my brother are in shock. So am I. The next few hours are a blur.

By that night, my parents, my brother, and their two dogs had moved in with me with nothing but the clothes they were wearing. The house, and the contents within, was a total loss.

I assumed the parental role of getting everything taken care of. I got them new clothing and replaced medications. I inventoried the items lost, which was everything they owned, for insurance. I worked with the builders to get the house re-built, and once completed, I worked with a realtor to sell it because they were no longer able to climb the stairs. I navigated insurance reimbursements. I did *all* of it. While changing jobs. Looking back, I know my Caretaker manager part took over and took charge.

Meanwhile, I shut down—again. When my Managers weren't engaged in my to-do lists and work, I binged food and Netflix for months, gaining back the weight and losing the fitness I had worked so hard to obtain.

I had spent a long time running away from being my parents. Then they moved in with me, and I found myself right back in all of my old habits. That didn't just bring out my Inner Critic, it supercharged it. And yet I couldn't bring myself to listen to it and get off my ass to do anything about it.

I was depleted—overweight, depressed, oppressed by my Inner Critic and unsure of what came next. Then I met Jess.

Jess ignited a spark in me, not just physically but emotion-ally, in ways I didn't fully understand at the time. The pattern was about to repeat itself, only with a much higher high and a much lower low.

Jess—The Coach Who Met My Inner Child

Jess is a life and triathlon coach. I had subscribed to her newsletter during my training days, for mental skills training for triathletes, but I never read them—until one day in the fall after the house fire. She was offering a Black Friday three-month coaching package, and it sparked an interest, so I signed up. I thought it would provide some accountability for me to get moving again and back to the healthier habits I had let go. Three months would be enough time for me to get momentum to fly on my own. It sounded like a good idea.

From the start, there was something uniquely different about Jess. She was mindful and present, and I was immediately drawn to her because she made me feel seen and cared for. My inner child attached in a similar way it did to Sharyn, only this time it was all in.

I soon found myself signing up for a year-long intensive coaching package. While still focusing on health and weight loss, there was a shift to self-awareness and personal growth, and I responded to her coaching in ways I couldn't have even imagined.

The depression lifted, and I was now wanting to reach new heights I never thought possible. If there was one word to describe Jess's impact on me, it would be "possibility." My parts that dig their heels in on change pulled back some, and all of a sudden life seemed like a wide-open canvas. It was exhilarating.

By the second year of working with Jess, I was hiking 14ers and cycling in Spain. All the while, I was emotionally attaching to Jess as a surrogate mother figure, completely unaware of the dynamic at the time.

Boundaries with Jess became blurred, and soon I was inviting her to concerts, staying at her house, and hanging out with her and her partner, Chad, as friends would. Just as with Sharyn, I found myself lost in Jess's energy rather than being in my own. After all, Jess's energy was so much more alive and fun than my damaged and numbed-out one.

I started working with Jess in early 2016. I was hiking, biking, doing races, and even starting to think about the possibility of exiting a job I thought I would be in forever.

Radiology was a career that suited me well when I was younger because it was a way to be a doctor but still hide myself. As I became more open from the personal growth, I realized the career no longer fit my needs. Additionally, the hospital practice I was in was toxic. Long hours and office politics made a job I didn't care for anymore even worse. I had two modes: working and recovering from work—and I felt trapped in it. Jess helped me open my mind to something different.

By mid-2018 I had quit my stressful hospital practice for a work-from-home teleradiology job. Even though I was still in radiology, the shift in practice was enough to rejuvenate me from the burnout, and I suddenly had the time and energy to entertain my dream of doing an Ironman. I had regained enough fitness by then that it was a realistic goal.

By late 2018, I had registered for Ironman Arizona, and the dream became a reality. I spent 2019 training and did a half Ironman in June. Then the push for Arizona began.

Jess sent me weekly training plans, and I followed them religiously. I wasn't fast, and it was not graceful, but I marched my way through months of grueling training—all the while, borrowing energy from the attachment I had to Jess. I was doing this training not only for myself; I was also doing it to please Jess.

Yes, I have parts that are people pleasers too, especially for people I attach to.

The emotion leading up to race day was palpable. I was ALIVE. I was attached, and the void was full for the time being. I was also about to do something I had dreamed of since that first short triathlon I did years before: Ironman.

Race day was even more emotional. It was mentally grueling and beyond physically demanding. But Jess was there with me every step of the way. While I didn't see her much on the swim or bike, she was a frequent face by the time I got to the run, which was the hardest part. Not only was it my weakest discipline, but it was at the end when the fatigue was at its worst. She encouraged me. She kept me apprised of my time. She warned me when I was going to have to speed up or miss the time cutoff. She helped me strategize, and when I made the decision that my night was over because I was not going to make the mile 17 time cutoff, she consoled me.

She was more than a coach to me that day. She was my nurturing presence. My emotional crutch. My friend.

The Felt but Unseen Wound

Shortly after my race, as we navigated what was next in our coaching relationship, I think we were both becoming aware of the blurred boundaries. The intense emotion of something like an Ironman will do that, I suppose.

Whatever the reason, Jess pulled back. I still remember a voicemail she left where she explained how, in no uncertain terms, we weren't friends. I was gutted. What? Not friends?

This wasn't just a rupture of a connection—this was cat-astrophic-level dumping. I rapidly spiraled into a depression. Looking back, it makes so much sense, because the rupture went right into my core wound of neglect and exploded it. I think it was the turning point in my journey. I hit rock bottom of the core wound and knew I couldn't continue this roller-coaster approach to life.

I jumped into other things. I became fixated on building a functional medicine practice and getting out of radiology entirely. I started working with a different, more business-minded coach. She was great, but I didn't attach to her like I did Jess. I am thankful for that because I still communicate with that coach in a healthy way. That distraction didn't last long, however, because within a few months of the rupture with Jess, I woke up one morning with tingling in my feet.

It was the beginning of the eventual MS diagnosis that rocked my world.

The Part I Hadn't Met Yet

It's a familiar story. Build myself up. Feel alive. Feel inspired. Attach to someone as a mentor who helps fill that lonely void. Crash and burn. Rinse and repeat.

Through every cycle, though, there was always a little spark in the back of my brain somewhere that wouldn't ever let me give up.

I didn't have a name for it, but in retrospect, I see that it was a part. I imagine a pilot light in the system that simply re-fused to go out no matter how hard the wind blew. It kept me getting out of bed on days I didn't want to. It kept me alive, really. It was curious. It never let go of the idea of there being something more to life—and to me. And it always maintained a sense of hope.

I have now come to know that little light as a part I call the Guardian—a high Self-like part that, in the face of an absent Self, ran the show.

Imagine a classroom full of rowdy and energetic eight-year-olds. There is a substitute teacher, so all the kids know they can be rowdy: standing on desks, throwing paper airplanes, yelling, running around, hitting each other, etc. The substitute teacher is trying hard to gain control and teach but can't seem to manage. Then the regular teacher returns and the class settles down. The kids are ready and eager to learn, and if not, at least still and quiet so others can.

My Guardian is like the substitute teacher who has worked tirelessly for years to teach a group of rowdy parts with little to show for it—except for the fact that it held space long enough for the real teacher, Self, to return.

As Self energy is returning, there is a tremendous sense of gratitude and awe for my Guardian. It has held the ship steady on a healing course all this time, fighting tides and currents, all the while quietly waiting for Self to return. This letter was written in a moment of that reflection.

Letter to my Guardian

> Hi. Self here. When I first decided to write to you, I wasn't sure what I should name you. I have called you Self-like because you have essentially been my surrogate for a long time. Someone needed to steer

the ship a little while I was away, and you took on that role in such a way that even you believed you were really me. That is dedication.

And I would like to mention curiosity. It is this quality that stands out. I wrote about you in this way before. You are the curious one, aren't you? The one who is always asking questions, always looking to see what is around the next corner, always seeking more. That truly has been the biggest contribution.

I have also called you the Clinician. Because you have spent so much time studying the healing process and have really guided it with the persistence and skill of a clinician—always reassessing diagnosis and prognosis.

The Watchtower is also a fitting name because you sit high up looking down on the rest of your siblings with the care and concern of a parent.

Ultimately, though, I think I will call you the Guardian. Because all your effort has really pointed to one objective: to guard over everyone until I returned. You have done that with such tenacity and skill that you deserve a fitting, regal name. I hope you like it.

We have reached that moment, though, where it is time for you to move over and sit in the assistant Guardian chair. I can steer the ship now. I can guard now. I can be curious and all the things. There may be times when I can't be around or just need help, and rest assured, I will call on you. Like a backup quarterback, I want you to be ready to step in when needed. But for now, get some rest.

Before we go any further, I want you to hear me say this plainly: I love you. You kept me alive. You kept everyone safe.

That will never go unrecognized. Pat yourself on the back for a job well done and watch the results of all of your effort start to spring forth. I have seen how hard you have worked over the years—how hard you have tried. I have seen how well-intentioned you are, albeit at times slightly misguided. That isn't on you. It's on me for leaving you alone to find the way.

You got us closer than I could have ever imagined, but we are still just a bit off course. As I do some slight course correction, I don't want you to go away or think about things that maybe could have been done differently. Instead, I want you to admire yourself for all the things that got us this far, and I want you to take notes on how this can be just a little easier for you moving forward.

In your curiosity , the central theme has been "How can I change things?" The question is a noble one because you saw how seemingly broken everything was and really tried so hard to make it better for everyone. You have been relentless in your pursuit of change, which is such an admirable quality.

You have managed to generate a lot of change in the pursuit—the most important of which is bringing me back and nursing me back to health to where now I am strong enough to take over. You could have settled for being the one in charge, but yet you kept going, knowing deep down inside that one day it would lead to losing your full-time job.

Some changes have been good. Some not so much, but all done with pure and noble intent. Change, though, isn't something that you can control as tightly as you thought. For now, take a break and rest in ease, knowing that I have you. Thanks for handing it over control in such good shape.

The ground you have tended is fertile for lasting change. It is more ready than ever for planting. And when you are ready, come back and join me—and although we cannot predict what and how they will grow, we can lay down seeds and navigate real change together.

The Guardian has been with me far longer than I ever realized. Before I had language for parts, before I knew what "Self" was, there was something inside me that refused to let me disappear completely. It's the part of me that signed up for an Ironman when everything in my life felt stagnant. It's the part that kept searching for meaning long before I knew how to define what I was looking for.

Even when I was deeply depressed, stuck in a career that felt hollow, and trapped in caregiving roles that were slowly draining me, the Guardian never left. It didn't shout. It nudged. It gently guided me toward the idea that there might be something more.

Even though I didn't officially meet this part or have a name for it until just recently, it has been there this whole time, propping me up. Of all the parts in my system, it may be the most important. It stood in for Self when I couldn't. It led when no one else could. And it kept me going in every moment when I felt like giving up.

And now, my Guardian can take a well-deserved rest and a bow—because there is a new sheriff in town.

Enter Self.

CHAPTER NINETEEN

The Emergence of Self

*The longing to be remembered and heard,
woven into the music of life.*

Self-Discovery

I called this chapter "Emergence of Self" rather than "Return to Self" because, on the one hand, my Self energy has always been there. On the other hand, due to infant trauma, Self never really had a chance to lead. I wasn't returning to Self; I was discovering it.

It might seem like semantics, but emerging Self energy has fueled my entire healing journey. Before I started ketamine therapy with Ashley, I had no idea that I was missing Self. I knew I was missing something, but I couldn't name it. My Guardian part has spent a lifetime trying to name it and find it.

Looking back I can see that during some of the highs in life, my Guardian was having success (with the aid of other Manager parts) at protecting me from the wounds that lay beneath, and my Firefighters could rest a bit. Things felt steady. And my Guardian took those opportunities to explore deeper places that set the stage for the work I am doing now. During lows, blows to the wounds would penetrate, and those Managers and Firefighters would come to the destructive rescue with things like dissociation, eating junk food, and shutting down.

But what was missing in all of those dynamics was Self.

While I was introduced to the concept of Self energy early on in my therapy with Ashley, it wasn't until I got more comfortable with ketamine sessions that I truly experienced it. The medicine sessions began to take on new life when Self energy started to emerge. The ketamine softened my protector parts just enough that the long-dormant Self could emerge and be known.

I had moments, brief at first, where I could feel a clear distinction between when I was in Self energy and when I was blended with other parts. And while it didn't last long, it left a lasting impression. When in Self energy I was also able to allow things like nurturing touch without parts objecting. Self, it turns out, really likes touch. As Self energy grew during ketamine sessions, I began to access it more between sessions, too.

Access to Self energy grew exponentially after a memorable group ketamine session. Even though I didn't have my own personal therapist at my side the entire time, there is something about being in a group that increases the energy and the depth of the work.

I also decided to do a larger dose of ketamine that day, which intensifies the experience, with an increased loss of reality. As I started to lose that grip on reality, Manager parts that like control started freaking out and anxiety ensued. Ashley came over to me and offered some touch, which at this point was starting to comfort me during sessions. However, I told her no, I didn't want it—not because I was averse to it, but because I could feel a sense of Self emerging. All of a sudden, I wrapped my arms around my torso in a big self-hug and started repeating, "I love myself, I love myself."

Ashley stepped away, but I kept saying, "I love myself." I don't know how long I repeated that phrase. After that ketamine session, things felt a bit different. Ashley noticed and commented that it seemed to be a pivotal point, and that ever since my Self energy was much more present.

What does Self energy feel like to me? I already described the Eight Cs of Self. IFS also describes Five Ps of Self energy: presence, perspective, patience, persistence, and playfulness.

I do experience many of these qualities when in Self energy; in fact, I'm in it now while creating this book. But beyond that, when I am in Self energy, there is a *feeling*. The best way to describe it is stillness. It isn't what I would describe as a positive feeling, but it's the noticeable absence of the anxiety and tension that show up when a part is leading.

My Guardian part possesses many of the same qualities of Self, especially curiosity, but I can often distinguish my Guardian from Self because sometimes the Guardian will get frustrated or stuck. Self doesn't have the quality of frustration. Sometimes it's subtle, sometimes it is in my face. And I still spend a lot of time in non-Self-led places, including where I'd rather not be, like eating a cupcake.

But Self energy is growing slowly, day by day. And the pathway home is now familiar.

Boundaries and Becoming

One of the effects of lack of Self energy is a blending of energy, not only with parts but also with other people. I've described how it felt trying to find myself while at the same time losing myself in the energy of others. Boundaries were nonexistent. I was parentified by my parents. I confused coaches for friends.

Without clear limits, being myself became impossible. My system was always looking to others, not in a healthy way that allowed for a defined sense of Self, but in a way that merged my energy with theirs. My spiral after my breakup with Jess is a prime example of how harmful that can be. Healthy boundaries allow for attachment while maintaining a solid sense of Self, rather than attachment with blending and loss of Self. While I had maintained boundaries with other therapists, it was because I didn't ever attach to them in the way I did to Sharyn or to Jess.

Ashley is the first therapist where attachment has not only been allowed and encouraged but has been essential to the work itself. Initially, I didn't understand this, and I started drifting toward the same line blurring that occurred with Jess. Ashley gently nudged me to help maintain a boundary I didn't know I needed. Early on, those nudges would cause me to fall into a shame spiral, feeling rejected. The spirals didn't last long, but enough for me to realize that this relationship was going to be different.

I had finally met a therapist that my parts wanted to attach to, but they didn't understand how to do that within the safety of a boundary. Looking back on that moment now, I see the brilliance in Ashley's responses and in the way she has held the boundary for both of us all this time. Ashley hasn't just helped me find my Self, she's guided me without inviting me to merge with her.

For the first time ever, I am in a relationship where attachment and connection deepen, but I don't disappear. I can show up as Self and stay there. And, as my Self energy grows, I am better able to set boundaries in other relationships. As I do that, some relationships are falling away.

Some have fallen away because I simply lost interest, while others have been harmful. Even though I'll always love her, it became clear that my friendship with Michelle was no longer good for me.

It takes time to build new relationships that are aligned with the Self. It's certainly taking some time for me. One of the key things Ashley provides is a stable and aligned relationship during this in-between phase where things can feel a bit lonely.

COMING HOME

"All That You Are"
—Goo-Goo Dolls

A recognition of brokenness and beauty, and the power of being loved as you are.

Until I began ketamine therapy, I carried a deep sense of not knowing who I was. I often said, "I don't know who I am," or "I don't know what I want."

As awareness of neglect and trauma grew, I went through a phase in which I lost what little sense of self I *did* have—and everything felt fake. I had lived through a trauma lens for so long, I didn't trust what was real. I didn't feel I could trust *anything* about myself.

But as the parts work within ketamine sessions deepened, something began to shift. I started to see that many of my parts —like the Comedian—*were* me all along. They weren't distortions; they were exaggerations.

Yes, I really *am* funny. My Manager part had simply magnified that aspect of my Self. Yes, I'm smart—my Analyzer ran with it. Yes, I'm kind and caring—my Caregiver part took that natural Self energy and went overboard. The emergence of my Self energy allowed me to feel like I was connected with who I was for the first time in my life.

But as with relationships, there is an in-between space here as well. As Self emerges, identities that wounded parts had attached to start to fall away, and there can be a fear that there isn't anything underneath them. As a result, it can be destabilizing.

But over time, Self qualities start to dominate more of the picture, and you find solid ground as the new identity, rooted in who you were *meant* to be all along. The question wasn't "Who am I?"; it was "*Where* am I?" I *did* know who I was all along. I just had to rediscover how to let those qualities be guided by Self, not driven by protection.

In Self, they are still there, but now they are natural, aligned, and integrated. Not reactionary. Not compensatory. Just . . . me.

And now that Self is in charge, I am better able to navigate the complexity of the parts in my system. Self continues to learn about them, hear their stories, and build trust.

Is Self always leading?

No.

Are there times when a Firefighter is in charge?

Yep.

But there is now a genuine remembrance of what coming home to Self feels like, and I can return there again and again when things spiral.

Healing is non-linear. It isn't two steps forward, one step back, like many say.

Now I ask this question: "Am I in Self energy, or is a part in charge?" That is the dynamic that influences the journey. It isn't backward and forward, which implies a "getting somewhere" in the equation. There is nowhere to go—but simply learning to *be*. It is a dance with your parts. And it's messy, but it is absolutely beautiful. It is a process of becoming that never ends.

CHAPTER TWENTY

Integration

"One Step Closer"
—Bon Jovi

A determined anthem of persistence and choosing to move forward again.

I have come full circle—from inner shitshow to Self. There has been a lot of beauty around a whole lot of mess. I have grown in ways I could have never imagined just a few years ago, despite already being on a journey of self-discovery.

The journey was slow moving until the diagnosis of MS in the fall of 2020 created a greater sense of urgency, shifting my focus to healing *it* rather than healing *me*. I didn't truly realize what "healing" truly meant until recently. Before, my only definition of "healed" was "no more MS."

I now understand that there is no "healed." There is no point where I'm going to say, "Okay, I'm good, and I can move on with my life."

Some of the wounds from my childhood will always be

there. It's about learning to soothe them when they surface. Over time, they bubble up less often, and when they do, they have much less impact.

I also realized that healing is developing a relationship with one's Self, a process that requires daily intentionality. Healing isn't a switch that flips from unhealed to healed. It is a lifelong relationship with Self—a continuum of baby steps, giant leaps, and occasional setbacks. It is non-linear and oscillating but always moving. I am not sure where it's all headed, but I know that wherever my parts and I are going, we are one step closer.

So as I arrive at the end of this book, I cannot say I am "healed." But I have been healing steadily since the first day I walked into Ashley's office three and a half years ago.

I have been introduced to a lot of ideas and modalities, all of which are described on the preceding pages.

They include psychedelic therapy, somatic therapy, emotional neglect, developmental trauma and cPTSD, attachment wounds and relational healing, and somatic memory.

Perhaps, though, the biggest contribution to my healing over the last few years is the introduction of IFS. I have met and befriended numerous parts. I have spent years building trust and cultivating relationship with them. And through it, I have come to understand myself a whole lot better than before. I have also learned what it feels like when Self is leading my parts.

I have met many Managers. The most important of which is my Guardian, who is Self like and without whom I would not be here writing this book. I have met Firefighters, including my food and suicide parts. These parts still show up at times. I have met several Exiles, including those from physical and possibly sexual abuse, but also my Tender One—the part that is shrouded in shame from emotional neglect. I am still in the process of unburdening these Exiles. It isn't a quick process. It's taking time to build trust and safety.

In the meantime, I am learning to simply stay with them. In a recent medicine session, there was a long period of time where I thought nothing was happening. And then I understood in that moment something important was indeed happening.

My parts were testing me to see if I could *stay* with them. So I did. Self in the lead, my parts paying attention. And for a short while, everything felt as it should be. Trust is building.

I spent a long time looking for that one thing that would shift me. But ultimately, what makes this story profound is how the blending of all the ideas in this book has created a unique mix of tools that have completely transformed who I am. It has been nothing short of alchemy at its finest.

Underneath it all, I have been blessed to have found a therapist who not only understands trauma but also brings relational healing to life in her office every week. And *that* is the most important thing of all.

It's fitting to end with one final letter to my parts. It speaks to where I have been and where I am going in my healing journey—one part at a time.

I WON'T LET GO

"I Won't Let Go"
—Rascal Flatts

*A promise to stay and support,
no matter how dark the road becomes.*

Dear Parts:

For a long time I was unaware of you—all of you, and the pain you carry. I know you tried to get my attention, but I could not hear you, see you, or feel you. Your attempts were always met with a cold silence. The one source you thought you could trust, the one place where love should come from unconditionally, and I was absent.

At times, not only were your cries ignored, but they were stuffed down further with punishing demands on you and the body you inhabit. There were big punishing things like Ironman races, but also daily small ones with poor care for the body and soul. Just as the world around you treated you with neglect and actual abuse, so have I. I understand that as time went on, your cries felt futile, and eventually you had to resort to the only thing you had left to try.

Although your physical manifestation started at a really young age with the extra weight, I could always push myself through that with restrictive eating and intense exercise. It allowed me to ignore it. Not only that, but I allowed the one part I COULD hear—the Inner Critic—to bully you about it without stepping in in your defense.

I can see how you had to resort to more extreme measures to get my attention. I have to admit, the MS is a brilliant strategy. It certainly did get my attention. Not in the way you intended initially. That took a while. But eventually, I was finally able to hear, see, and feel some of you for the first time.

I have been with some of you awhile now, and I have noticed that the MS, and for that matter the weight, have not improved. In fact, both have gotten much worse since I started talking with you. I expected you to respond more than you have. But I also now have a much bigger understanding of just how hurt some of you are.

I also now understand that I am just now meeting some of you. The parts that are hurt the most have been the most deeply buried, and I get that it is those parts that carry many of the physical symptoms that ail me.

As I start to turn toward you—the parts I am just beginning to know—I want to take a moment to reflect on all of you. There is no need to respond— but if you do want to say something, I am listening.

To my Guardian: Thank you for getting me here. Without your persistence, resilience, and curiosity, I would not be here. You have been the steady presence in my absence, and I feel like we are going to have a beautiful working relationship moving forward into a new phase of healing.

To my Skeptic: I know you have your doubts still, but I feel them softening. For that, I am grateful. I got a message from some deeply hidden and shy parts that they cannot be known until they can be believed. I feel that you are close to allowing the belief. Keep listening—you are getting it, one message at a time. You can still call bullshit, but understand that nothing any of your siblings or I say is bullshit. Let's keep that label for the craziness going on around us.

To my Historian: We are in uncharted water here. There isn't anything in your history book about where we are headed. This isn't a status quo cycle. This is an open-ended, one-way path forward to places we have never been. Now that I am leading, you can rest on the fact that things ARE different already and that the cycle has already been broken. Keep recording, but let go of the past. It doesn't belong in our future. Healing does.

To my Comedian: I am so glad I have gotten to know you more formally. I have sensed you over the years but lately I really feel like I understand you better. I appreciate you and the humor and lightheartedness you bring to some of the darkest places I go. As I dive deeper into to those dark places, I am going to need you by my side to lighten the load. But I want you to understand that there is a time and a place for humor. Sometimes, things just have to feel dark and heavy.

To my Firefighters and Inner Critic: I know you guys are still at odds a lot of the time. I feel it. But please continue to work on a peace treaty. Allow me—Self—to take the head seat at the negotiation table. Peace can only come with an unbiased mediator, and I am here to help you understand each other. You are all striving for the same goal, and I intend to keep trying to help you see that.

To my Exile in the chest: I am so sorry you were hurt so badly. Suffocation is an unbearable trauma, especially when there is no one to save you from it. I am here now—and I am starting. I hope my presence allows you to trust enough to start breathing again.

To my Tender One: Oh, my most precious and tender Exile, you have carried the wound of being unseen and unloved as your entire existence. I try but still cannot completely imagine that pain. I see some of it: the shame, the meekness and desire to be invisible, and the anguish of loneliness. I hope now that you are seen and loved that the anguish and shame can begin to dissolve and you can emerge to fully embody that carefree and playful little girl you were always meant to be.

To my Exile in my pelvis/gut: I only recently met you. My understanding of you for now, is limited. I sense you but cannot fully see or hear you. I know that you don't trust me enough to be fully seen—not yet anyway. But I also am thankful that there is some small amount of trust that allowed you to let yourself be seen, even if briefly and in subtle ways. I don't know what happened to you, and I want you to know that it's ok if you never tell me. But I DO want you to know that regardless, you are seen and you are safe. And you are so loved. I trust that you will emerge in your own timing and when you do, I will be here. If you want me to feel your pain, I'll feel it. If you want me to hear your cries, I'll listen to them. And if you just want to say nothing, I'll stay with you anyway.

Finally, to all the parts I have not met yet, the parts who don't fully trust yet, the parts that haven't fully unburdened yet, and the parts who hold my physical ailments. And specifically, I want to include the parts that I know live in my legs—and that hold so much pain that you carry MS. I promise you I am going to keep going until I have met you, gained your trust, and helped you unburden. Whatever it takes, I will do; I'll do more ketamine sessions where you feel more fully seen and more journaling where you can be heard. More quiet times where we can just sit together. I'll keep writing to you. But most of all, I will stay. I will love you.

To the parts I have met – and to all the ones I haven't yet
To Dobby
To My Self:
I won't let you go.
Love always,
Kim

EPILOGUE
Where I Am Now

"Roads"
–Chris Mann

*A reflection that every road we travel —
with scars and battles — always leads us home.*

If healing is on a continuum, where am I on it now? The short answer? Somewhere in the middle: better than I used to be, but not yet where I want to be.

Emotionally, the last three years have been a roller coaster. Currently, I feel more emotionally well than I ever have. My Inner Critic isn't gone, but I have so much more capacity for self-compassion than ever before, enough that I can finally say I love myself for the first time in my life.

I have set boundaries. I am better at saying no. I even distanced myself from my best friend of twenty years because it was an emotionally harmful relationship. I am learning to be in a relationship without losing myself in it. I am learning who I am through all of it. Embracing it. All of it—the darkness and the light.

And while it is easy to have regret and wonder how different my life would have looked without the trauma, I realize that my experiences are what have brought me here. I don't think I would have so much awareness without those experiences, including the MS, because I would not have had a reason to look within.

I don't necessarily believe everything happens for a reason. But I do believe that making meaning out of what happens can be a blessing in disguise. I still at times wonder what things would be like if I had a "normal" childhood. Would I have a family? Would I be a musician rather than a radiologist? Would I be the model of health?

But I had a different experience, and I can't change it. What I *can* change is me. And I am well on my way to doing that, and for that I am truly grateful.

Emotionally, I'm stronger than ever. Physically, though, the healing lags behind. I started therapy a few years ago with a focus on healing MS. Since then, the MS symptoms have actually gotten worse, and I have gained weight.

It is a bit disappointing that the physical health and the emotional healing seem to be on different trajectories. But there are a few reasons why this could be true.

I have woken up my trauma. I have tapped into stored emotion. Yet, I have not yet unburdened my exiles. That is a work in progress. As I intentionally feel my wounds, it is only natural that my food Firefighter has been active. My eating habits haven't always been about health but about soothing pain. I'm learning to negotiate with that part so that I can return to eating for nourishment rather than comfort.

In radiology, pneumonia is often still visible on a chest X-ray long after the patient feels better. There can be a lag between what the image shows and the person's actual health. In the same way, only in reverse, healing could be happening in me, even if the symptoms lag behind.

For all of these reasons, and possibly more, I have hope that my physical health will shift. I just have to be patient. This isn't a quick or easy process. I learned that early on.

Spiritually, I have moved from seeking to connecting. I don't feel a deep connection, but there are sparks. And I have found some peace with the nagging ache of finding purpose. My purpose is to heal and to share my experience. I have found myself in my writing.

I still have a long way to go before I feel I've arrived. I still have the stories. I still have music. And all my parts are here. But now, Self is here. Becoming is learning to return to Self over and over again.

And I am becoming—every single day. No matter what road I find myself on in life, they will always lead me back home.

And no matter where you are on the continuum, know this: you are not behind.

Healing isn't a race, and there's no finish line to cross. Wherever you are is exactly where you need to be.

You are not broken.

Only becoming.

Becoming is the work.

Becoming is the *gift*.

ACKNOWLEDGMENTS

"Kind and Generous"
—Natalie Merchant

*A song of gratitude for the generosity
and love of others.*

My therapist, Ashley. I had no idea how blessed I was to have found her when I first walked through her door. She has been a quiet, steady presence throughout this journey. And while I may be the one at the center of this story, I would not be here without her.

From a clinical perspective, her knowledge already exceeds many in her field, and she continues to grow with unwavering commitment—both as a therapist and as a human.

She understands that healing requires more than one modality. She knows her role is not to lead but to hold space until the real leader, the client's Self, can emerge. She also understands that healing calls for more than therapy techniques; it demands attunement and presence. These are gifts she offers with rare consistency and skill.

Looking back now, I can see the brilliance in how she brought all of this into our work. For a long time, I didn't even realize what she was doing. I didn't understand attunement. I didn't understand the role of relationship. But she was there, quietly in it with me all along. And when I reflect on how it's unfolded, the timing has been perfect.

I often think of her as my own personal Mr. Miyagi. If you were born after 1990, the reference might be lost on you; you should watch *The Karate Kid*.

Over the last three years, I've been learning "wax on, wax off" in the form of somatic work, touch therapy, parts work, nervous system regulation, emotional regulation, trauma repatterning, attachment repair, boundary setting, embodiment, and relational capacity. All while slowly cultivating trust, not just in Ashley, but in myself.

Now it feels like I'm in the tournament, and everything is coming together into one seamless, unified skill. Only instead of trying to win a karate match, I'm learning that "waxing" was never a means to an end. It was the point all along.

I have Ashley to thank for that. And yes, I still have parts that say "This is stupid" and "This is bullshit" every time she sits beside me or puts her arm around my shoulder. But my Self is proud to admit that I'm attached. Ashley, if you're reading this—I want a hug at my next appointment.

I will forever be grateful.

Mindy has been my guide for psilocybin journeys, and I've met with her both online and in person for preparation and integration. She is a highly intuitive and skilled therapist, always showing a palpable enthusiasm for my growth.

While Ashley remains my primary therapist, Mindy has brought a fresh perspective that has proven invaluable. Her care and presence during six- to eight-hour medicine journeys, some of which have been incredibly challenging, have made a lasting impact. I'm deeply grateful to have her as part of my support team.

Melanie is a more recent addition to my support team. At Ashley's request, she has joined several ketamine/PSIP sessions to support relational dynamics that benefit from the presence of two people. I've also met with her individually when Ashley was unavailable or after medicine sessions for integration. Like Mindy, Melanie is deeply intuitive and insightful. She brings in fresh, timely reflections that consistently support and deepen my process.

My Inner Critic has commented more than once on how ridiculous it is that I have three therapists. But that's an easy one to rebuff. Each has played a unique and meaningful role, and I feel incredibly lucky to have them in my corner.

In addition to psychotherapy, both traditional and medicine-assisted, I've also leaned on a variety of complementary support tools. These have included bodywork, acupuncture, sound healing, Sufi healing, spiritual direction, and group programs like an MS embodiment course. Some of these supports have been steady companions; others were brief encounters that nonetheless left an impression. All have contributed something meaningful to my journey, and I would be remiss not to mention them, even if only in broad terms.

There are a few people I'd like to specifically acknowledge.

Stacy Cadenhead has been a consistent presence on my team, offering massage therapy, sound healing, and a safe space to process out loud. Her reflections are steady and nonjudgmental, and I've always felt met in her presence.

Megan Evans, a fellow traveler with MS, introduced me to powerful embodiment practices through her program, MS Stage.

Lorie Wilson has been a quiet force in my healing, always reminding me that the heart leads the way. Her gentleness creates a space where I can fully open, every time I'm on her table.

I'd also like to thank former mentors, coaches, and friends. Some have come and gone, some still by my side—all impactful.

To Jess:
My former life and triathlon coach. While our relationship was marked by blurred boundaries, I carry no blame—only sincere gratitude for the time I spent under your wing. With you, I soared to heights I never thought possible. The lessons from that season, whether uplifting or difficult, have shaped me in lasting ways. Without them, I would not be where I am today. Every step of this journey has been necessary.

To Sharyn:
Thank you for being a mentor and a role model in fitness and health. And thank you for always believing in me even when I didn't. You led by example and it has had a lasting influence.

To Anne:
You know who you are. "People like us find each other." Thank you for always being just a Voxer message away from a laugh

and for the Eckhart Tolle reference after my meditation retreat. That shift in perspective was exactly what I needed. Keep flying high.

There are many others who've played small but meaningful roles in my story. I'm grateful for every one of them.

To my friends: Thank you for putting up with me. All versions of me.

To Beth:
To a fellow medicine traveler, albeit on separate paths. Thanks for being someone who "gets it" when talking about the medicine sessions and always being a supportive sounding board. Most of all, thanks for being a fellow dog mom. Wheeler and Lexi are probably playing together in that big pasture in the sky, talking about how much their moms loved them and each other.

To Bethany:
There are no words, really. You have been a friend, an assistant, a personal chef, a cheerleader, a confidant, and most of all, you have been a light that always shines bright. Even though you have many reasons to feel victimized, you always show up for life, and I wish nothing but good things for you. Let your soul continue to shine. Or in other words, KEEP THAT SHIT UP! Love you!

Lastly, to my dear friend **Jo Swayne:**
I've known you since my freshman year of college—more than

half my life. We've witnessed many versions of each other across all kinds of seasons, but the current version of our friendship is perhaps the most cherished. As I extend my relational growth beyond Ashley's office and into real life, you have been a steady, grounding presence. I've shared things with you in ways that have made me feel seen. And for the first time, even with a longtime friend, I feel safe being fully myself. Thanks for being you—and for always reminding me to CTFD.

APPENDIX A
More on Psychedelics

Psychedelic Therapy

There are a variety of psychedelic medicines, each with unique qualities. I have used a combination, including ketamine, MDMA, and Psilocybin. Others include cannabis, ayahuasca, and LSD. The differences in how these drugs work are beyond the scope of this book. I do think it's important, however, to point out a few features that will help give context for the reader.

Ketamine is a man-made drug that is FDA approved for anesthesia. It can be administered as an oral troche (dissolved in the mouth), as an injection, or intravenously. I did the oral troches for my first few experiences, but the majority of my journeys have been via intramuscular injection. Ketamine is not technically a psychedelic but has psychedelic-like properties. It is dose-dependent. Smaller doses are considered psycholytic, where the dose is just enough to soften the protector parts and allow access to deeper material/parts. The higher the dose, the more psychedelic the experience. At super high doses, ketamine becomes an anesthetic. It is, by nature, a dissociative agent, and for people with dissociation, it can make it challenging to stay present and embodied during the session. I have done a variety of doses and have had a variety of experiences. If you are starting ketamine therapy, it may take some experimentation to find a dose that is the sweet spot for working with parts and/or PSIP. Ketamine journeys are shorter. One dose tends to last less than forty-five minutes or so. In my journeys, we do multiple doses to extend the journey, but in total, it's still less than two hours.

MDMA is a synthetic drug, also known as ecstasy or Molly. It is generally ingested in a capsule. An MDMA journey will last longer—anywhere from four to eight hours. One of the unique qualities of this drug is that it stimulates the release of oxytocin, which is the body's "love" chemical. It also reduces activity in the amygdala, which is the brain's fear center. So a journey with MDMA typically results in a more loving and connected experience. Difficult material may arise, but there is some separation from the associated fear and/or anxiety.

Psilocybin is a natural compound found in a variety of mushrooms. It is typically ingested as the dried mushroom or in a tea. The journey can last anywhere from six to eight hours. Psilocybin is a more organic and embodied experience than ketamine and can be a bit harsher emotionally than MDMA. While a psychedelic experience can vary widely from person to person and from journey to journey, my experience is that psilocybin goes much deeper. The emotional access during a psilocybin journey is much more visceral than with ketamine or MDMA. It is not uncommon to combine MDMA with psilocybin to go deeper into difficult material and have the warm sense of connection that MDMA can provide.

It's important to acknowledge something practical here too: accessibility.

Ketamine therapy is legal in all fifty states but is rarely covered by insurance, making cost a real barrier for many. Psilocybin and MDMA, while showing great promise in research, are still illegal in most places, which means sessions can only happen in limited, supervised contexts. I was fortunate: my career in radiology provided me the financial resources to pursue this kind of work. Many people don't have that access. It's one of the reasons I feel so strongly about sharing my story. Healing should not be reserved for those who can afford it. My hope is that as laws and policies evolve, these medicines will become more available—and more affordable—for the people who need them most. In the meantime, I want to stress that Internal Family Systems and PSIP do not require psychedelics to be effective. These modalities stand powerfully on their own; medicines simply softened the edges enough for me to get there faster.

APPENDIX B
Song List

How to Read This Book

"Symptom of Being Human"—Shinedown

Introduction

"The Calling"—Mary Chapin Carpenter

Meet the Characters: My Parts

"I Dare You"—Shinedown

Chapter 1: Running On Empty

"Unstoppable"—Sia

"She Used to Be Mine"—Sarah Bareilles

"Rock Bottom"—Citizen Soldier

"Be Slow"—Harrison Storm

Chapter 2: The Moment Everything Changed

"Watershed"—Indigo Girls

"A Safe Place to Land"—Sarah Bareilles, John Legend

"Easy On Me"—Adele

"This Is Your Life"—Switchfoot

"Maybe"—from "Annie"

"Bitter Ender"—Mary Chapin Carpenter

Chapter 3: Internal Wars—Conflicting Parts

"Monsters"—Shinedown

"Schizophrenic Conversations"—Staind

"I Am Light"—India Arie

Chapter 4: From Thinking to Feeling

"Breathe Me"—Sia

"Floating Through Space"—Sia, David Guetta

"Movement"—Hozier

**Chapter 5: Meet My Exiles—
Hello from the Prison of Pain**

"Hello"—Evanescence

Chapter 6: Touch and Connection

"Grow as We Go"—Ben Platt

"All I Want"—Kodaline

**Chapter 7: From Connection to Rupture and the
Tender Exile Underneath**

"You Say"—Lauren Daigle

"Satellite Call"—Sarah Bareilles

"I'm in Here"—Sia

**Chapter 8: Love, Intimacy, and Desire—
The Deepest Layer of Shame**

"Iris"—Goo Goo Dolls

"And So It Goes"—Billy Joel

"Show Me"—Idina Menzel

"Passionate Kisses"—Mary Chapin Carpenter

Chapter 9: Pleasure Belongs Here

"Soak Up the Sun"—Sheryl Crow

Chapter 10: This Is Bullshit!—My Hardworking Skeptic

"Doubt"—Twenty One Pilots

Chapter 11: Change: The Gas and the Brake

"December"—Sarah Bareilles

"Happy"—NF

"Hope"—Shinedown

"Courage to Change"—Sia

"There's Always One More Time"—BB King; Harry Connick Jr.

Chapter 12: Layers

"My Skin"—Natalie Merchant

"This Is Me"—Kesha, from *The Greatest Showman*

Chapter 13: The Eternal Dance of Jekyll and Hyde—Who's in Charge Today?

"Hi Ren"—Ren

Chapter 14: The Chameleon and the Void

"What's It Gonna Take"—Sarah McLachlan

"Who I Am"—Wyn Stark

Chapter 14 Vignette:

"Survive"—Lewis Capaldi

Chapter 15: Home Is a Song

"Home Is a Song"—Mary Chapin Carpenter

"I've Got the Music in Me"—Heart

"Chameleon"—Herbie Hancock

"Scars in Heaven"—Casting Crowns

"Bird Set Free"—Sia

APPENDIX C
Emotional Neglect Questionnaire

(From *Running on Empty* by Jonice Webb, PhD)

Circle the questions to which your answer is yes.
Do you:

1. Sometimes feel like you don't belong when with your family or friends

2. Pride yourself on not relying on others

3. Have difficulty asking for help

4. Have friends or family who complain that you are aloof or distant

5. Feel you have not met your potential in life

6. Often just want to be left alone

7. Secretly feel that you may be a fraud

8. Tend to feel uncomfortable in social situations

9. Often feel disappointed with, or angry at, yourself

10. Judge yourself more harshly than you judge others

11. Compare yourself to others and often find yourself sadly lacking

12. Find it easier to love animals than most people

13. Often feel irritable or unhappy for no apparent reason

14. Have trouble knowing what you're feeling

15. Have trouble identifying your strengths and weaknesses

16. Sometimes feel like you're on the outside looking in

17. Believe you're one of those people who could easily live as a hermit

18. Have trouble calming yourself

19. Feel there's something holding you back from being present in the moment

20. At times feel empty inside

21. Secretly feel there's something wrong with you

22. Struggle with self-discipline

Look back over your circled YES answers. These are windows into the areas in which you may have experienced emotional neglect as a child.

These are some of the books that most influenced my healing journey. Each offered me language, tools, or simply the sense that I wasn't alone. If any part of my story resonates with you, you might find these books helpful companions, too.

If you're not sure where to start, the five books that made the biggest impact on me are noted with a double asterisk.

****Jonice Webb – *Running on Empty* (2012)**

The book that first gave me words for "emotional neglect." It describes what it feels like to grow up without obvious abuse but still with an ache you can't explain—and how to begin healing.

Jonice Webb – *Running on Empty No More* (2017)

A follow-up that explores how emotional neglect plays out in adult relationships and how awareness can open the door to connection.

****Pete Walker – *Complex PTSD: From Surviving to Thriving* (2013)**

A practical and compassionate guide to understanding cPTSD, especially emotional flashbacks, the inner critic, and the life-long patterns neglect can create.

Pete Walker - *The Tao of Fully Feeling: Harvesting Forgiveness Out of Blame* (2002)

This book focuses on reclaiming our right to feel deeply, especially emotions like anger, grief, and shame that are often suppressed after trauma. It's less of a structured recovery manual and more of an invitation to embrace emotional authenticity.

****Richard C. Schwartz - *No Bad Parts* (2021)**

The essence of Internal Family Systems in an accessible, powerful book. If you want to understand why I talk to my "parts," start here.

Richard C. Schwartz & Martha Sweezy - *Internal Family Systems Therapy*, 2nd ed. (2020)

A more clinical book, but still approachable if you want to dive deeper into the model behind my letters and conversations with parts.

Richard C. Schwartz - *Greater Than the Sum of Our Parts* (2019)

An audio-friendly, experiential guide with meditations for connecting to your inner world.

****Bessel van der Kolk - *The Body Keeps the Score* (2014)**

A modern classic on how trauma lives in the body and how healing must involve more than just talk.

Peter Levine - *Waking the Tiger* (1997) and *In an Unspoken Voice* (2010)

Both helped me understand the language of the body and why somatic work is so essential for trauma healing.

Gabor Maté - *When the Body Says No* (2003)

The first book that helped me connect the dots between chronic illness (including my MS) and unprocessed emotions.

Gabor Maté - *In the Realm of Hungry Ghosts* (2008)

Focused on addiction, but equally relevant to anyone who's used coping strategies to numb pain.

****Gabor Maté with Daniel Maté - *The Myth of Normal: Trauma, Illness, and Healing in a Toxic Culture* (2022)**

A sweeping look at how trauma and chronic stress are woven into the fabric of modern life. Maté argues that what we often call "normal" in Western culture is actually profoundly unhealthy—and he offers a path back to authenticity, wholeness, and healing.

Linda Metcalf & Tobin Simon - *Writing the Mind Alive* (2002)

Introduces the proprioceptive writing practice I stumbled upon before therapy—a method that helped me start hearing my Exiles before I had words for them.

Jeff Brown - *Soulshaping* (2010)

A memoir about trauma, spirituality, and self-discovery. It gave me permission to believe that my own story mattered.

Paul Knitter - *Without Buddha I Could Not Be a Christian* (2009)

A thoughtful exploration that helped me reconcile spirituality beyond rigid doctrine.

Joe Dispenza - *Breaking the Habit of Being Yourself* (2012)

More cerebral and science-based, but it opened a doorway for me to think differently about energy, belief, and possibility.

"Could Have Been Me"
—The Struts

*A fiery anthem about living fully,
with no regrets about what could have been.*

KIM TAYLOR is a physician, endurance athlete, and trauma survivor whose healing journey led her beyond the limits of conventional medicine and into the world of deep inner work. After facing a series of physical and emotional breaking points—including an MS diagnosis, caregiving burnout, and the collapse of old coping systems—Kim turned inward.

Through Internal Family Systems (IFS), ketamine-assisted psychotherapy, Psychedelic Somatic Interactional Psychotherapy (PSIP), and somatic-based therapy, Kim began to map the complex landscape of her inner world—one part at a time. Writing became her way in.

In this debut work, Kim shares her story not as a therapist, but as someone who's done the hard work of healing from the inside out. Her letters, reflections, and raw accounts of transformation offer a unique perspective for anyone navigating trauma, dissociation, attachment wounds, or the longing to reconnect with the Self.

She lives with her rescue dog, Dobby, and continues to explore what it means to belong to herself.